MANAGING PERSONAL BANKRUPTCY

AND ALTERNATIVES TO BANKRUPTCY
IN THE UNITED KINGDOM

DAVID MARSH

Editor: Roger Sproston

Emerald Guides

Emerald Guides

978-1-913776-74-9

Printed by 4edge www.4edge.co.uk

Cover design by BW Studio Derby

Whilst every effort has been made to ensure that the
information contained within this book is correct at the time of
going to press, the author and publisher can take no
responsibility for the errors or omissions contained within.

Contents

PART ONE.
THE PERSONNEL INVOLVED IN BANKRUPTCY IN ENGLAND AND WALES AND THE DEBT RESPITE SCHEME

Introduction

Chapter 1-The Personnel Involved in Bankruptcy-England and Wales   **17**
The Insolvency Service   17
Modernised Insolvency Rules   17
What the Insolvency Service does   19
The Official Receiver   20

Chapter 2-The Debt Respite Regulations 2020   **23**
General information   23
Creditors responsibilities   24
Debt advice providers   25
The role of the Insolvency Service   25
Starting a breathing space-Applying for a standard
breathing space   25
Applying for a mental health crisis breathing space   26
Debtor eligibility for a standard breathing space
Debtor eligibility for a mental health crisis breathing
space   27
Information the debt adviser needs   27
Qualifying debts   29
Excluded debts   30
Request to not disclose debtor's address   31
When a breathing space starts   32

What to do during a breathing space   33

Taking action on the notification   33

If you have sold the debt on   34

Debts identified after a breathing space starts   35

Stopping enforcement action   36

Appointed agents   38

Existing legal proceedings   39

Where a court judgment or order has not yet been issued 39

Where a court judgment or order has been issued   40

Contact between creditors and debtors during a breathing 41
space

Creditor access to the breathing space register   42

Receiving payments during a breathing space   43

Ongoing liabilities during a standard breathing space   44

Cancelling a standard breathing space   45

Cancelling a mental health crisis breathing space   46

Breathing space cancelled after creditor review   48

Breathing space not cancelled after creditor review   48

Apply to court to cancel a breathing space   48

If you do not comply   48

End of a breathing space   49

When a mental health crisis breathing space ends   50

End of a breathing space notification   50

PART TWO
ALTERNATIVES TO BANKRUPTCY-ENGLAND AND WALES

Chapter 3- -Debt Management Plans   **55**

Structuring a Debt Management Plan   57

Making payments   59

Debt management Plans and Credit status 59
Companies offering a free Debt Management Plan
service: 60

Chapter 4-Individual Voluntary Arrangements **61**
How IVA's work 61
Key components for a successful IVA 64
Advantages of an IVA-Individual, partner or sole trader 64
Disadvantages of an IVA 64
Companies offering IVA advice 65

Chapter 5-Administration Orders **67**
Who is eligible to apply for an Administration Order? 68
Debts 69
No longer able to afford payments? 70
Administration Order paid off? 70
Companies offering advice on Administration Orders 71

Chapter 6-Debt Relief Orders **73**
What is a debt Relief Order? 73
Who can apply for a debt relief order? 75
Type of debts included in a debt relief order 75
Your assets 76
Those ineligible for a debt relief order 76
Applying for a Debt Relief Order 77
Things not to do before applying for a DRO 78

*

PART 3

THE PROCESS OF BANKRUPTCY ENGLAND AND WALES

Chapter 7-The Process of Bankruptcy-England and Wales 83

Fast-Track Voluntary Arrangement (FTVA)   83
Costs of the FTVA   84
Duration of the FTVA   84
Bankruptcy   85
Advantages of going bankrupt   85
Disadvantages of going bankrupt   85
PARV order   86
How to apply   86
Debts that bankruptcy covers   87
Which debts are included in bankruptcy?   87
Mortgages and bankruptcy   88
Debts you took out by fraud   88
Debts in joint names   89
Business debts   89
More information   89
How to go bankrupt   89
Dealing with the official receiver after bankruptcy   91
What the official receiver does   91
Interview   91
Public examination   92
Creditors' meeting   93
Income payments agreement   93
Bankruptcy restrictions orders   96
What is a BRO?   97
Extra restrictions   97

Other consequences of a BRO 98

Getting a bankruptcy cancelled 98

When can bankruptcy be cancelled? 98

Effects of cancelling bankruptcy 99

How you apply to cancel bankruptcy 100

If you've paid your debts and expenses in full 100

If the bankruptcy order shouldn't have been made 100

If your creditors have agreed an IVA 101

Accessing your bank account after going bankrupt 102

Opening a new bank account 102

If you've been refused a bank account 102

Basic bank accounts 103

Post Office card account 103

Prepaid debit card 104

Your home 104

Pension rights 105

Your life insurance policy 106

Your wages 106

Restrictions on a bankrupt 106

Ending bankruptcy 107

Debts 108

Assets that you obtained or owned before your discharge 108

Assets you obtain after your discharge 108

Debts incurred after you have been made bankrupt 109

Credit reference agencies 109

Checking the information on your credit file 110

Making a complaint 110

*

PART 4

SCOTLAND AND NORTHERN IRELAND

Chapter 8-Bankruptcy and Alternatives to Bankruptcy in Scotland **113**

Coronavirus - more protection from action by creditors 113

Changes to Bankruptcy rules in Scotland 114

Sequestration in Scotland 115

Alternatives to Sequestration 118

Minimal asset process (MAP) bankruptcy 118

Who can apply for MAP bankruptcy? 118

How MAP bankruptcy works 119

Trust deeds 119

What is a trust deed? 119

Protected Trust Deed 120

Voluntary Trust Deed 120

Benefits of a Trust Deed 121

Disadvantages of a Trust Deed 121

Securing a trust deed 122

Obligations under a Trust Deed 122

Full cooperation with the trustee. 123

Debt Management Programme 123

Debt Arrangement Scheme 124

What kinds of debt can be included in a DAS? 124

How does a DAS work? 125

Advantages 126

Disadvantages 127

Business Debt Arrangement Scheme (BDAS) 127

Useful addresses 127

Chapter 9-Bankruptcy and Alternatives to   **129**
Bankruptcy in Northern Ireland
Becoming bankrupt in Northern Ireland   129
Filing your own bankruptcy petition   129
A creditor making you bankrupt   131
Alternatives to bankruptcy   131
Where is a bankruptcy order made?   132
Who deals with your bankruptcy?   132
How bankruptcy affects you   133
Assets   133
Earnings   133
Ongoing commitments   134
Other applications   134
Your obligations when you're bankrupt   134
How long does bankruptcy last?   135
Useful information and advice   135

Glossary of terms
Useful Addresses and Websites
Index
Example forms to be used in Bankruptcy

Introduction

Over the last ten years, personal bankruptcies and company insolvencies in the UK have risen to record levels, in large part to do with the economic climate, also the steady rise in personal debt. At the time of writing, we have been through the worst period on record due to COVID 19. In 2021 there has been a significant rise in both personal debt, bankruptcies and insolvencies. It is said that the worst is yet to come. Also, It is not clear how BREXIT will affect the future, if at all. For sure many companies have struggled since the UK's exit from the EU in 2021.

Personal debt in 2021

More people are opting for alternatives to bankruptcy and are going for IVA's (Individual Voluntary Arrangements). People are also opting for Debt Relief Orders, which are cheap to enter into but apply only to those with less than £15,000 in unsecured credit debts and under £1000 in assets. In addition, pensioners, once a negligible part of the whole picture, are increasingly having to seek relief from debt.

Since COVID 19 there has been a huge increase in personal debt, as a result of company failures and job losses and it is to be expected that there has been an enormous backlog of work for the practitioners. During the period when it was impossible to interact with the various agencies involved, the government brought into a series of payment holidays, such as mortgages and credit cards. However, as these tail off so will the number of people in need of help increase.

The Debt Respite Scheme 2021

The Government has introduced new regulations In the form of The Debt Respite Scheme (Breathing Space Moratorium and Mental Health Crisis Moratorium) (England and Wales) Regulations 2020 which came into force on 4 May 2021,

The Debt Respite Scheme (Breathing Space) will give someone in problem debt the right to legal protections from their creditors. There are two types of breathing space: a standard breathing space and a mental health crisis breathing space. A standard breathing space is available to anyone with problem debt. It gives them legal protections from creditor action for up to 60 days. The protections include pausing most enforcement action and contact from creditors and freezing most interest and charges on their debts.

A mental health crisis breathing space is only available to someone who is receiving mental health crisis treatment and it has some stronger protections. It lasts as long as the person's mental health crisis treatment, plus 30 days (no matter how long the crisis treatment lasts).

We will be discussing the new regulations in full in Chapter 2 as they provide important respite for debtors. In this chapter, I will discuss the regulations in detail, including information that will be of use to both creditors and debtors. It should be noted that the Regulations cover England and Wales only.

This wide-ranging book, which covers personal bankruptcy and alternatives to bankruptcy, deals firstly with the personnel involved in bankruptcy, then covers alternatives to bankruptcy and also personal bankruptcies in England and Wales-recognising that bankruptcy is the last and final option to solving debt problems.   Bankruptcy and alternatives to bankruptcy in Scotland and Northern Ireland are also covered.

Overall, this is a very practical book and will benefit all who need further advice in this complex area in this challenging time.

****

PART ONE.

THE PERSONNEL INVOLVED IN BANKRUPTCY IN ENGLAND AND WALES AND THE DEBT RESPITE SCHEME

Chapter 1

The Personnel Involved in Bankruptcy-England and Wales

Bankruptcy in the United Kingdom is divided into separate local regimes for England and Wales, for Northern Ireland, and for Scotland. There is also a UK insolvency law which applies across the United Kingdom, since bankruptcy refers only to insolvency of individuals and partnerships. Other procedures, for example administration and liquidation, apply to insolvent companies. However, the term 'bankruptcy' is often used when referring to insolvent companies in the general media.

The Insolvency Service

The Insolvency Service, which is an executive agency of the Department of Business, Innovation and Skills, operates under a statutory framework-mainly the Insolvency Acts 1986 and 2000, Amended by the Enterprise Act 2002, the Company Directors Disqualifications Act 1986 and the Employment Rights Act 1996. New rules have been introduced from April 2017 (see below)

The website which answers all queries is:

www.gov.uk/government/organisations/insolvency-service

Modernised Insolvency Rules

The new rules guide insolvency practice from April 2017. Modernised and consolidated insolvency rules have been laid in

Parliament and came into force on 6 April 2017. The new rules replace the Insolvency Rules 1986 and their 28 subsequent amendments. They have been developed working with the insolvency profession and have been approved by the Insolvency Rules Committee.

The rules have been recast to reflect modern business practice and to make the insolvency process more efficient.

Changes include:

- enabling electronic communications with creditors
- removing the automatic requirement to hold physical creditors meetings, although creditors will be able to request meetingsenabling creditors to opt out of further correspondence and for small dividends to be paid by the office holder without requiring a formal claim from creditors

The rules apply in England and Wales. In Sotland, the introduction of The Insolvency (Scotland) (Company Voluntary Arrangements and Administration) Rules 2018 and The Insolvency (Scotland) (Receivership and Winding up) Rules 2018 (together the 2018 Rules) will bring about the biggest overhaul to insolvency law in Scotland since the introduction of the Insolvency (Scotland) Rules 1986 (the 1986 Rules) over 30 years ago.

The 2018 Rules largely imitate those brought in by the equivalent England and Wales legislation, the Insolvency (England and Wales) Rules 2016 (the England and Wales Rules).

General

As of 2021, there is a network of 22 Official Receiver offices throughout England and Wales with 1,700 staff. The Enforcement Directorate and headquarters are in London, Birmingham, Manchester and Edinburgh.

What the Insolvency Service does

The Insolvency Service will:

- administer bankruptcies and debt relief orders
- look into the affairs of companies in liquidation, making r reports of any director misconduct
- investigate trading companies and take action to wind them up and/or disqualify the directors if there is evidence of misconduct act as trustee/liquidator where no private sector insolvency practitioner is in place
- issue redundancy payments from the National Insurance Fund
- work to disqualify unfit directors in all corporate failures
- deal with bankruptcy and debt relief restrictions orders and undertakings
- act as a impartial source of information for the public on insolvency and redundancy matters
- advise BEIS ministers and other government departments and agencies on insolvency and redundancy related issues
- investigate and prosecute breaches of company and insolvency legislation and other criminal offences on behalf of BEIS

If you are thinking about going bankrupt you can contact the Insolvency Service via their website. The national helpline on National Helpline on 0300 678 0015 is. Alternatively you can go to the Citizens Advice website citizensadvice.org.uk, full address contained in the back of this book. The National Debtline also provides useful information nationaldebtline.org.uk 0808 808 4000.

The Official Receiver

The Official Receiver is a civil servant in the Insolvency Service and an Officer of the Court. He or she will be notified by the court of the bankruptcy or winding up order. He/she will then be responsible through their staff for administering the initial stage, at least, of the insolvency case. This stage includes collecting and protecting any assets and investigating the causes of the bankruptcy or winding up.

The Official Receiver's staff will contact you, either immediately if action is urgently needed or within 2 days of receiving an insolvency order or bankruptcy order. Usually they will arrange an appointment for you to attend the Official Receiver's office for an interview, normally within ten working days of receiving the order from the court. He or she will then act as your trustee in bankruptcy unless the court appoints an insolvency practitioner to take this role. Assuming that it is the Official Receiver who will be acting as your trustee, he or she will be responsible for looking after your financial affairs during your bankruptcy and also your financial affairs prior to you being made bankrupt.

If the Official Receiver does not require you to attend an interview you will be sent a questionnaire to fill in and return.

See chapter six for the detailed process of bankruptcy and the steps involved.

In the following chapters we will look at the alternatives to bankruptcy in England and Wales. The alternatives are Debt Management Plans, Individual Voluntary Arrangements, Administration Orders and Debt Relief Orders.

****

Chapter 2

The Debt Respite Scheme (Breathing Space Moratorium and Mental Health Crisis Moratorium) (England and Wales) Regulations 2020

The new Debt Respite Scheme 2020 is a very important piece of legislation, which needs to be understood in the light of the escalating debt problems which have arisen as a result of the pandemic. The scheme deals with mental health and well as financial debt. Chapters 3-5 cover alternatives to bankruptcy-it is crucial to undestand the new regulations when deciding which route to take. The below explains the scheme in detail and how to manage it

The (The Debt Respite Scheme (Breathing Space Moratorium and Mental Health Crisis Moratorium) (England and Wales) Regulations 2020 Breathing Space) came into force on 4 May 2021,

The Debt Respite Scheme (Breathing Space) will give someone in problem debt the right to legal protections from their creditors. There are two types of breathing space: a standard breathing space and a mental health crisis breathing space. A standard breathing space is available to anyone with problem debt. It gives them legal protections from creditor action for up to 60 days. The protections include pausing most enforcement action and contact from creditors and freezing most interest and charges on their debts.

A mental health crisis breathing space is only available to someone who is receiving mental health crisis treatment and it has some stronger protections. It lasts as long as the person's mental health crisis treatment, plus 30 days (no matter how long the crisis treatment lasts).

Creditors responsibilities

As a creditor, if you're told that a debt owed to you is in a breathing space, you must stop all action related to that debt and apply the protections. These protections must stay in place until the breathing space ends.

The electronic service will send you a notification to tell you about each debt owed to you in a breathing space and the date the breathing space started. You need to make sure you apply the protections to these debts from the date set out in the notification.

If you're a creditor, it's also possible your debt might be added to a breathing space at a later date, because it is only identified after the breathing space has started. In this case, you have to apply the protections from the date you get the notification, or when the regulations consider you to have received it, whichever is the earliest.

For electronic notifications this is the date they are sent. For postal notifications this is 4 working days after it was posted. If you have any questions about a breathing space you've had a notification for, you should contact the debt advice provider whose details are in the notification.

Debt advice providers

A breathing space can only be started by:

- a debt advice provider who is authorised by the Financial Conduct Authority (FCA) to offer debt counselling
- a local authority (where they provide debt advice to residents)

Debt advice providers are responsible for the administration of a breathing space. They are the point of contact for the debtor, their creditors (and appointed agents), and the Insolvency Service (who own and maintain the electronic service).

The Insolvency Service

The Insolvency Service maintains the electronic service that debt advisers use to start the breathing space process, and they send notifications to creditors during it. They also maintain a private register of:

- details of people whose debts are in a breathing space
- the date a breathing space ended or was cancelled in the last 15 months

Starting a breathing space-Applying for a standard breathing space

Debtors can only access a breathing space by seeking debt advice from a debt adviser. Anyone who cannot or is unlikely to be able to repay their debts can apply to a debt adviser for a standard breathing space. Although all applications must be considered, the debt adviser might decide a breathing space is not appropriate for a debtor.

For example, if a person could pay their debts with some budgeting help, or they already have assets that could easily be sold to clear the debt, a breathing space would not be the right solution. A breathing space might also not be appropriate for a someone who can enter a more suitable debt solution straight away, without needing the protections.

Applying for a mental health crisis breathing space

The government committed to develop an alternative route to access the protections for people receiving mental health crisis treatment, so that they do not have to access debt advice first. If an Approved Mental Health Professional (AMHP) certifies that a person is receiving mental health crisis treatment, the AMHP's evidence can be used by a debt adviser to start a mental health crisis breathing space. In addition to the debtor, the following people can apply to a debt adviser on behalf of a debtor for a mental health crisis breathing space:

- any debtor receiving mental health crisis treatment
- the debtor's carer
- Approved Mental Health Professionals
- care co-ordinators appointed for the debtor
- mental health nurses
- social workers
- independent mental health advocates or mental capacity advocates appointed for the debtor
- a debtor's representative

Debtor eligibility for a standard breathing space

Before a debt adviser can start the breathing space, they must confirm their client is eligible and meets all the conditions. These are that the debtor must:

- be an individual
- owe a qualifying debt to a creditor
- live or usually reside in England or Wales
- not have a debt relief order (DRO), an individual voluntary arrangement (IVA), an interim order, or be an undischarged bankrupt at the time they apply
- not already have a breathing space or have had a standard breathing space in the last 12 months at the time they apply
- The debt adviser must also be satisfied that their client meets both of the following conditions:
- their client cannot, or is unlikely to be able to, repay all or some of their debt
- a breathing space is appropriate for their client

Debtor eligibility for a mental health crisis breathing space

The debtor must still meet the same criteria and conditions for a standard breathing space, but they must also be receiving mental health crisis treatment at the time that an application is made. A debtor who has had a standard or mental health crisis breathing space in the last 12 months may be eligible for a mental health crisis breathing space. There is no limit to how many times a debtor can enter a mental health crisis breathing space.

Information the debt adviser needs

To apply, a debtor must provide their debt adviser with their:

- full name
- date of birth
- usual residential address (in some very limited circumstances, this address might be withheld from the breathing space register and any notification to creditors)
- details of the debts that they owe, including the type of debt they owe
- the name and contact details for the creditor
- if relevant and known, the name and contact details for any agent appointed by the creditor

- If the debtor is a sole trader and has business debts to include, they must also provide:
- their trading name or names
- any business address

Debt advisers will also try to find out and provide extra information that might help you identify the debtor or their debt. This might include:

- the debtor's previous names and addresses, if they've recently changed
- details of any amounts or references relevant to the debt (such as the debtor's National Insurance number, if the debt is a government debt, or a credit card number)

However, this information is not required before a debt adviser can start a breathing space. A debtor must have at least one qualifying debt owed to a creditor, and this must be included in the application. The debtor must tell the debt adviser about all of the debts they know about and give them the contact details they have for each creditor. If they know about a debt collection agent acting on a creditor's behalf, they might also give the debt adviser those details. This does not change the legal standing of either the agent or the creditor.

Qualifying debts

Debts included in a breathing space must be qualifying debts. Debts are any sum of money owed by the debtor to you, while liabilities are any obligation on the debtor to pay money to you. Most debts are likely to be qualifying debts. These will include:

- credit cards
- store cards
- personal loans
- pay day loans
- overdrafts
- utility bill arrears
- mortgage or rent arrears

Government debts like tax and benefit debts are all likely to qualify, unless they are included in the list of excluded debts. Joint debts can be included in a breathing space, even if only one person applies for a breathing space. The joint debt would become a breathing space debt, and you must apply the same protections to the other people who owe that debt to you. The breathing space does not affect the other people's debts and liabilities in their own names.

While guarantor loans can be included in a breathing space, the protections do not extend to the guarantor. The guarantor can apply for their own breathing space, if they're eligible. Qualifying debts can include any that the debtor had before the Breathing Space legislation came into force on 4 May 2021. New debts incurred during a breathing space are not qualifying debts. Neither are new arrears on a secured debt that arises during a breathing space.

Excluded debts

All personal debts and liabilities are qualifying debts, except for:

- secured debts (like mortgages, hire purchase or conditional sale agreements). You can only include arrears on these debts that exist at the date of an application for a breathing space. Any new secured debt arrears that happen after the breathing space starts are not protected. If a secured debt is also an ongoing liability and a debtor misses payments, it could mean the debt adviser stops their breathing space
- debts incurred from fraud or fraudulent breach of trust. You should think of this in the same way you would if a person is bankrupt. Discharge from bankruptcy does not release a person from bankruptcy debts which they incurred by fraud. If you request a review of a breathing space because of fraud or suspected fraud, you might have to provide evidence to the debt adviser or to a court
- liabilities to pay fines imposed by a court for an offence. This includes any interest on the fine and any penalties connected to it. This does not include penalty charge notices, like a parking ticket
- obligations from a confiscation order

- child maintenance or obligations under an order made in family court proceedings
- a crisis or budgeting loan from the social fund
- student loans
- damages they need to pay for death or personal injury caused to someone else
- advance payments of Universal Credit
- council tax liabilities have not yet fallen due. If all instalments for that financial year have fallen due and have not been paid, these are considered to be a qualifying debt. If a debtor has been served with a 'reminder notice' to pay a council tax bill, the remaining liability for the financial year is a qualifying debt

While some business debts also qualify for the breathing space, they do not qualify if the debt only relates to the business (not the debtor personally) and the debtor is VAT registered, or the debtor is a partner in a business with someone else. An eligible non-domestic rates debt (or business rates) is a qualifying debt if all instalments for that financial year have fallen due and have not been paid. If a debtor has been served with a 'further notice', the remaining liability for that financial year is a qualifying debt.

Request to not disclose debtor's address

When applying for a breathing space, a debtor or their representative can ask their debt adviser to withhold their usual residential address from you. The address can be withheld if it is reasonably expected that showing the address would lead to violence against them or someone who normally lives with them. If the debt adviser decides that the debtor's address should be withheld, it will not appear in any notifications sent to you and will not be on the register maintained by the Insolvency Service.

When a breathing space starts

A breathing space will start the day after the debtor's details are put onto the breathing space register. If you receive electronic notifications about the start of a breathing space, you should receive a notification the same day that details are put on the register. It's likely this will be the day before the breathing space starts. If you receive notifications by post, it's likely you'll receive it after the breathing space has started.

Once a debtor's details have been put onto the register, you'll receive a notification, telling you the breathing space start date and details of your qualifying debt (if the debt adviser had those details). If the debt adviser is aware that you are owed more than one qualifying debt, you will receive a notification for each debt. 'Taking action on the notification' has advice on what to do if you are not sure which debt or debts the notifications relate to. You can receive notifications by:

- electronic communication (either a notification directly from the electronic service or an email). We can only send electronic communications to you if you opted in through the electronic service
- post
- someone leaving a copy of the notification at your address
- The regulations consider that you've received:
- an electronic notification on the day it was sent

- a postal notification 4 business days after the notification was posted
- a notification left at your address on the day it was left

What to do during a breathing space
Taking action on the notification

When you receive a notification, you must search your own records to identify the debt owed to you by the debtor. This needs to happen as soon as possible. If you have only received notification about one debt, but you are owed two debts (for example, the debtor has an overdraft and credit card debt with you) then you should consider applying the protections set out below to both debts and, in all cases, you should tell the debt adviser about the additional debt. It is the debt adviser who will decide if the additional debt qualifies for the breathing space. You must make sure you stop:

- the debtor having to pay certain interest, fees, penalties or charges for that debt during the breathing space
- any enforcement or recovery action to recover that debt, by you or any agent you've appointed
- contacting the debtor to request repayment of that debt, unless you've got permission from the court

Interest can still be charged on the principal in secured debt, but not on the arrears. If it's not possible to stop interest, fees, penalties or charges accruing on the debt during the breathing space (for example, this could be because of IT system limitations), it can continue to accrue. However, the debtor must not be required to pay charges or interest that accrue in this way either during or after the breathing space.

Nothing in the regulations changes what a customer is contracted to pay. For example, if a payment is due during the breathing space and it includes interest that would have been due normally, creditors are not expected to make complex system changes to recalculate these payment amounts. Instead, creditors can make an adjustment to the overall balance owing on the debtor's account as soon as they can.

Ideally, communications you send debtors should not show interest, fees or charges that accrue during a breathing space. However, it does not breach the regulations to show them, as long as you do not require the debtor to pay. You must make sure you are not asking the debtor for payment. You might want to tell the debtor how you'll deal with this accrual during the breathing space. You can contact the debtor with information about how you will deal with their breathing space.

If you have sold the debt on

If you receive a notification of a breathing space debt that you have sold to another creditor (an 'assigned creditor'), you must tell that creditor the breathing space has started and give their contact details to the debt adviser. If you do not do this as soon as possible, you're liable for any losses the debtor or the assigned creditor have as a result.

If you've told a debt adviser the contact details of the assigned creditor, they must update the details on the electronic service. You will not receive any more notifications about that debtor or the debt, and you will not be able to view any of those details on the electronic service. If you are the assigned creditor, the original creditor should tell you about the breathing space. From the date the breathing space started, you must stop any interest and fees on the debt from being charged and any enforcement action. You will receive a notification from the electronic service, which will tell you what action to take.

Debts identified after a breathing space starts

When you receive a notification, you must search your records for details of the debt you've been notified about. You must also search for any additional debts owed to you by the debtor. If you find an additional debt, or it is not clear which debt the notification is about, you must tell the debt adviser about it as soon as reasonably practicable. What is reasonable may depend on the nature and complexity of your systems, records and processes or the type of debt or liability owed by the debtor.

When the debt adviser is given (or becomes aware of) details of an additional debt, they must decide whether it is a qualifying debt. If the debt adviser decides that it is, they must update the electronic service. The electronic service will send you a notification. The additional debt does not become a breathing space debt until the debt adviser has updated the electronic service and a notification has been sent to the creditor. You do not need to apply the protections to this debt until you receive the notification or it is considered in the regulations that you have received the notification, whichever is the earliest (the day it was sent if you receive it electronically or 4 days after posting). However, this will not change the original start or end date of the breathing space.

The exception to this is where the debt adviser is told of the additional debt more than 45 days after the breathing space started. In these circumstances, it's possible the debt adviser might think it's not appropriate to add the additional debt to the breathing space and can decide not to do so.

If the debt adviser decides not to add the additional debt to the electronic service, you will not receive any notification about the debt from the electronic service. In these cases, you can continue any action to recover the debt. If you notified the debt adviser about an additional debt but have not had a notification about the start of a breathing space for it, you should contact the debt adviser dealing with the breathing space to confirm what is happening.

Stopping enforcement action

Once a breathing space has started, you or anybody acting on your behalf must not take any enforcement actions against the debtor or anyone who is jointly liable with them for a breathing space debt. Enforcement action is when you try to:

- collect or enforce a breathing space debt, including where this is done by any agent you've appointed. This includes the Department for Work and Pensions (DWP) where they are collecting a breathing space debt on your behalf through third party deductions. It does not include an existing attachment of earnings order made before the start of the breathing space, which may continue
- apply to DWP for a new third party deduction to be taken from an individual's benefit payments
- try to enforce a judgment or order issued by a court or tribunal, before or during the breathing space, without the court's permission
- enforce your security over a breathing space debt
- obtain a warrant or writ

- get or seek a liability order

- sell or take control of the debtor's property or goods. If a bailiff or enforcement agent has taken control of any goods by removing them and securing them elsewhere before a breathing space started, the goods may be sold during the breathing space and the costs of the sale deducted from the proceeds. However, fees accrued during the breathing space for storage of those goods cannot be charged either during the breathing space, or after it ends

- start any action or legal proceedings (including bankruptcy petitions) against the debtor

- make an application for a default judgment for a claim for money against the debtor

- take steps to install a pre-payment meter or use a pre-payment meter already installed for the supply of gas or electricity, to collect payment for a debt in the breathing space, unless the debtor has already provided their consent to do so, before the breathing space starts

- take steps to disconnect a debtor's premises from a supply of gas or electricity, unless they have taken that supply illegally

- serve a notice to take possession of a property let to the debtor on the grounds of rent arrears due up to the start of the breathing space; or take possession of a property let to the debtor having served such a notice prior to the start of the breathing space

- contact the debtor about the enforcement of a breathing space debt. The only exception to this is where you are required to contact or engage with the debtor under the Consumer Credit Act 1974, or by the FCA Handbook

Appointed agents

If you are notified that a debt has gone into a breathing space, you must tell any agents you've appointed or instructed to recover it. You must tell the agent to stop enforcement action. If you do not do this as soon as possible, you may be liable for any losses the debtor or the agent have as a result. If the debtor gives the debt adviser contact details for any agent appointed by a creditor when the debtor applies for the breathing space, a notification of the start of the breathing space will also be sent to the agent. If the agent is sent this notification, a creditor is not liable for any of the agent's losses they could have avoided. Where an agent manages the debt on behalf of a creditor, they should tell the creditor of the breathing space and the protections.

During a breathing space, any agent you have appointed or instructed must not:

- take enforcement action regarding the breathing space debt
- give notice about collecting or enforcing that debt
- visit the debtor's home or business to take their goods
- take any of the debtor's goods
- sell any of the debtor's goods, unless the agent took them before the breathing space started. If a bailiff or enforcement agent has taken control of any goods by removing them and securing them elsewhere before a breathing space started, the goods may be sold during the breathing space and the costs of the sale deducted

from the proceeds. However, fees accrued during the breathing space for storage of those goods cannot be charged either during the breathing space, or after it ends

- collect a breathing space debt through existing third party deductions from an individual's benefit payments
- seek to collect a breathing space debt by applying to DWP for a new third party deduction to be taken from an individual's benefit payments
- It is possible that the debtor will only give the debt adviser details of an agent, not of the original creditor, and that only the agent managing the debt is notified of the breathing space. If you are an agent that has been appointed to manage debt on behalf of a creditor, and you receive a notification, you will want to inform the creditor of the breathing space as soon as possible.

Existing legal proceedings

If you had already filed a petition for bankruptcy or started any other action in a court or tribunal relating to a debt that is now in breathing space, you must tell the court or tribunal in writing. You must do this as soon as you receive notification of the breathing space.

Where a court judgment or order has not yet been issued

Any court that receives notification about a breathing space debt where a bankruptcy petition has started, must stop the bankruptcy proceedings, until the breathing space ends or is cancelled. Other court proceedings about the debt (other than enforcement of court judgments or orders) can continue until the court or tribunal makes an order or judgment.

Where a court judgment or order has been issued

Unless the court or tribunal gives you permission to continue, the court or tribunal must make sure any action to enforce a court order or judgment about a breathing space debt stops during the breathing space. These might be actions like:

- holding a hearing during the breathing space

- making or serving an order or warrant, writ of control, writ of execution or judgment summons

- instructing an enforcement agent to serve an order, warrant, writ of control, writ, execution or judgment summons

The court or tribunal can still send notices or correspondence to the debtor about an action or proceeding.

Court orders and judgments for a breathing space debt, which were made before the breathing space began, cannot be enforced until the breathing space ends. This is unless the court or tribunal gives permission for these actions to continue.

Existing legal proceedings can continue when the breathing space ends. If a time limit for enforcement or new legal claims related to the debt ran out during the breathing space, this is extended to 8 weeks after it ends. You can still start or continue any legal action relating to any debt that is not a breathing space debt, during a breathing space.

Contact between creditors and debtors during a breathing space

Generally, during a breathing space, you (or any agents you have instructed) must not contact a debtor about any collection or enforcement action for a breathing space debt. This includes asking them to pay or starting or continuing any legal action. During the breathing space, you can contact the debtor's debt adviser about the debt you are owed, or to discuss a debt solution. You, or any agent, can only contact the debtor:

- about anything not related to the breathing space debt, like ongoing liabilities or an excluded debt
- if the debtor asks you to talk about a breathing space debt or a debt solution
- to respond to a query or complaint the debtor sent you
- about any action or legal proceedings the court or tribunal have allowed
- if you or your agent are required to do so under the Consumer Credit Act 1974 or by the FCA Handbook

These restrictions are intended to stop contact that reinforces the message that the debtor owes money to you or that they need to make payment. These communications can be worrying to debtors. It is not intended to stop communication that might be helpful to the debtor. You might want to contact a debtor at the start of a breathing space to tell them they do not need to worry about normal communications you send them. This might be particularly important if there are debts governed by the Consumer Credit Act 1974, where you're legally required to send them communications.

Any communication you send should be minimal and must be carefully drafted to make sure it could not be read like it is about asking them to pay what they owe. If you receive calls from customers worried by letters they receive from you during a breathing space, this may mean that you need to consider whether the letters are appropriately worded, and whether they are consistent with the regulations.

Contact between creditors and debt advisers during breathing space

You and the debt adviser may contact each other during the breathing space on anything about the debtor and your debt. This might include things like:

- a breathing space debt
- a debt solution for the debtor
- telling them about an additional debt
- asking for a review
- telling them the debtor is not meeting their obligations

You will need to consider your own data protection obligations and decide what action you might need to take where you are sharing personal data. The regulations make clear that the duty to disclose information under the breathing space scheme should be taken into account in determining whether doing so would contravene data protection legislation. The Data Protection Act 2018 permits you to disclose personal data to a third party where you are required to do so by law.

Creditor access to the breathing space register

We will maintain a private register with details of:

- the debtor's full name
- the debtor's date of birth
- the debtor's usual residential address
- the trading name or names and any address, if the debtor has carried on business with qualifying debts included in the breathing space
- the debtor's breathing space debts
- the date the breathing space started
- the date the breathing space ended or was cancelled
- If you have received a notification about a breathing space debt, you're allowed to see any information on the register about that debtor and the breathing space debt they owe to you. You are not able to see any information held about:
- any other creditor the debtor has
- any other breathing space debt owed to another creditor
- the debtor's usual residential address if it has been withheld

Receiving payments during a breathing space

A breathing space is not a payment holiday. While you cannot enforce a breathing space debt during a breathing space or charge interest or fees on it, a debtor is still legally required to pay their debts and liabilities. During the Breathing Space, the debtor should continue to pay any debts and liabilities they owe you. You can continue to accept these payments.

If there is a controlled goods agreement in place with an enforcement agent on a qualifying debt and a repayment plan has been agreed between the debtor and the enforcement agent, the debtor should continue to make payments under that agreement as they fall due. Although no enforcement action may be taken during the moratorium period and any time limit within the plan will be extended until 8 weeks after the end of the moratorium period, when that time limit expires, any unpaid instalments may be treated as a breach of the repayment plan.

Ongoing liabilities during a standard breathing space

Certain debts are considered 'ongoing liabilities' during a standard breathing space. The debtor needs to keep paying these if they can. If they don't, the debt adviser might cancel the standard breathing space. An ongoing liability is any payment the debtor has to pay during a standard breathing space for:

- a mortgage secured against the debtor's primary residence (this does not include arrears accrued up to the start of the breathing space)
- a lease or rental agreement for the debtor's primary residence (this does not include arrears of rent for the property accrued up to the start of the breathing space)
- an insurance agreement
- any taxes, duties and national insurance contributions
- any local taxes or rates for local authorities
- water, sewerage, electricity, gas, heating oil or solid fuel bills

Any other debts or bills (secured or unsecured) that fall due during a standard breathing space are not ongoing liabilities.

If a debtor does not pay ongoing liabilities during a standard breathing space

Where a debtor does not pay an ongoing liability, the debt adviser might decide to cancel the standard breathing space. The debt adviser will consider whether cancelling it is unfair or unreasonable to the debtor. This can be done as part of the midway review process. This obligation and review process does not apply to debtors during a mental health crisis breathing space.

Debt adviser midway review during a standard breathing space

During a standard breathing space, a debt adviser must carry out a midway review between day 25 and day 35. This is to make sure they are satisfied the debtor is complying with their obligations. If the debt adviser thinks the debtor has been meeting their obligations and communicating with them, the standard breathing space will continue until the end date. If the debt adviser thinks the debtor has not met all of their obligations, they can cancel the standard breathing space in respect of some or all the debts.

If you have asked for a review of a Breathing Space, the debt adviser might combine this with the midway review.

Cancelling a standard breathing space

Provided they do not consider that the debtor's personal circumstances would make it unfair or unreasonable, the debt adviser must cancel a standard breathing space for one or more of the related debts after carrying out a midway review if they consider that:

- the debtor has not met one or all of their obligations. This includes them not paying their ongoing liabilities (unless the debt adviser considers that the debtor did not have the financial means to do so)
- they have put a debt solution in place
- they have not been able to communicate with the debtor about their breathing space. This includes where the debtor is not contactable or is not available

- there is an issue with the debtor's application, or there has been some unfair prejudice to the creditor's interest, after completing a creditor's request for a review
- If the debt adviser decides it's necessary to cancel a standard breathing space after a midway review, they should discuss this with the debtor before it's cancelled, where they can. They must then:
- notify the debtor that the breathing space is being cancelled
- update the electronic service to tell the Insolvency Service the breathing space has been cancelled
- Updating the electronic service automatically updates the breathing space register. The cancellation takes effect on the following day. The electronic service will also send notifications to the creditors telling them the date of the cancellation and the reason the breathing space was ended.

Cancelling a mental health crisis breathing space

- A mental health crisis breathing space does not have a midway review, but the debt adviser will regularly check that the person is still receiving mental health crisis treatment. The mental health crisis breathing space will continue for the duration of this treatment, plus 30 days.
- However, the debt adviser must cancel a mental health crisis breathing space if:
- they believe the evidence provided to them about the debtor's mental health crisis treatment contains inaccurate, misleading or fraudulent information, and they do not consider that the debtor's personal circumstances would make the cancellation unfair or unreasonable

- the debtor asks for the mental health crisis breathing space to be cancelled

- **Request a breathing space review**
- You can ask a debt adviser to review the breathing space, or specific debts being included in it, only if you consider that:
- the breathing space unfairly prejudices your interests. For example, you think that there has been discriminatory treatment in respect of you, or your debt
- the debtor does not meet at least one of the eligibility criteria for a breathing space
- any of the debts included in the breathing space do not qualify
- the debtor has enough funds to repay their debts
- You have limited time to request a review, either:
- within 20 days of the breathing space starting, based on the start date in the notification you received
- within 20 days of an additional debt being added to the breathing space, based on the date when you received or were deemed to have received the notification

To request a review, you need to give the debt adviser a written statement with the reasons you want a review and provide any supporting evidence you want to provide. This will need to be done outside of the electronic service.

The debt adviser can decide to carry out the review you have requested as part of the breathing space midway review process.

The debt adviser must cancel the breathing space in respect of all or some of the debts if they agree with you unless the debt adviser thinks cancelling the breathing space is unfair or unreasonable due to the debtor's personal circumstances.

Breathing space cancelled after creditor review

If a debt adviser decides to cancel a breathing space after a creditor request for a review, they will update the electronic service to tell the Insolvency Service it has been cancelled. You'll receive a notification that the breathing space has been cancelled, and whether this is for some or all of the debts. After you have received this notification, you can restart enforcement action and charges. You cannot backdate any interest or fees accrued during the breathing space period, unless a court lets you.

Breathing space not cancelled after creditor review

If the debt adviser decides not to cancel the breathing space, they will tell you about this decision. The breathing space continues, but you can take further action by applying to a court, if you still do not agree.

Apply to court to cancel a breathing space

After a review, if you do not agree with a debt adviser's decision, you can apply to a court to cancel the breathing space in respect of some or all of the debts. You need to apply to the court within 50 days of the breathing space starting, or 50 days after being notified about an additional debt being added to it. You cannot do this before the debt adviser has completed their review and has let you know the outcome.

If you decide to apply to the court, you should tell the debt adviser. You must make the application based on the same reasons you sent to the debt adviser for your original review. The court will consider your case and tell you, the debtor, and the Insolvency Service of its decision. If the breathing space is cancelled for all of the debts or just some of them, the Insolvency Service will update the breathing space register. You will receive a notification that the breathing space has been cancelled, and whether this is for some or all of the debts.

You cannot backdate any interest, penalties, fees or charges accrued during the breathing space period, unless a court lets you.

If you do not comply

You must apply all the breathing space protections for a debtor after you're notified about a breathing space. If you do not, any action you take is null and void and you may be liable for the debtor's costs. The debtor can complain to their debt adviser, who will contact you to remind you of your obligations. The debtor can also complain directly to you, using your complaint procedure. This might include referring their complaint to any external ombudsman, oversight body or regulatory body.

If you still do not meet your obligations, the debt adviser can tell the Insolvency Service and we'll contact you to remind you of your obligations. Repeated breaches of the regulations can be considered by your regulator, where appropriate.

End of a breathing space

When a standard breathing space ends

A standard breathing space ends:

- 60 days from the date it started
- the day after a debt adviser or a court cancels it
- if the debtor dies during the breathing space period. In this case, the breathing space ends on the day after the debtor died

When a mental health crisis breathing space ends

A mental health crisis breathing space will end either 30 days after the debtor's mental health crisis treatment ended, or 30 days after the date a debt adviser had no response after asking for confirmation from the nominated point of contact about a debtor's ongoing mental health crisis treatment.

End of a breathing space notification

When a breathing space ends, you will be sent a notification. It will tell you the date the breathing space ended. If the breathing space was cancelled by the debt adviser or the court, or the debtor has died during the breathing space period, the notification will tell you the reason why it was cancelled.

Next steps

- When a breathing space ends, you can:
- start applying interest, fees, penalties and charges to the debt from the date that the breathing space ends. You cannot backdate or apply any interest, fees, penalties or charges that accrued or would have accrued during the Breathing Space period, unless a court allows you to do this
- take any action to enforce your debt, including contacting the debtor

- start or continue any legal proceedings about your debt

You cannot take these actions if the debtor has gone into a debt solution. This could include a debt relief order or bankruptcy. You also cannot take action if they have made a formal arrangement with their creditors to deal with their debt, such as an individual voluntary arrangement. You can check the Individual Insolvency Register to see if your debtor is in a formal insolvency solution.

****

PART TWO
ALTERNATIVES TO BANKRUPTCY-
ENGLAND AND WALES

Chapter 3

Debt Management Plans

Having discussed the new breathing space regulations, it is now time to discuss alternatives. A Debt Management Plan is a way of planning your debt payments over a number of years. It has similarities to an Individual Voluntary Arrangement in that it is a way of organising and paying off debt and keeping creditors at bay. There are two types of Debt Management Plan:

- The type where you are provided with standard letters and you are in charge of making payments. With this method you are in charge of dealing with your creditors.
- The type where a third party contacts all your creditors. Using this method, your financial situation is illustrated by a set of papers called a common financial statement. You will be represented by a third party and given 24hr support.

Whichever way you go, the end result is to control your debts. *Debt management plans have no legal standing and are not ratified by a court, as is an Administration Order for example.*

A debt management plan can provide solutions for the following:

- Those with unsecured debts that they cannot afford to pay

- Those with equity in their properties but who would rather not re-mortgage or take out a loan

- Those who do not qualify for an IVA, i.e. those with debts under £12,000

- For people who want a short term solution to debts i.e. those who are about to sell a home

- People who don't want to deal with their debts but would rather a third party take this on.

Essentially, a Debt Management Plan places your debt with a third party who deals with your debts on your behalf. Debt Management Plans are far more effective than taking out unregulated loans with very high rates of interest. It is very important to remember that debts with underlying security in them cannot be put into a plan.

Examples of unsecured borrowing

- Personal loans

- Overdrafts

- Credit cards

- Student loans

- Store cards

Secured debts are where the lender has a legal charge over some property of yours, so that if you default on payments, they can possess that property and sell it to get their money back.

Generally...The length of time that the debt management plan runs will depend on the way it is structured. A simple approach is to divide your monthly payments into your debts and that is the number of months that the plan will run. When organising the Plan you should concentrate on the priority of your debts. A priority debt is one which can have serious results if not paid, such as mortgage, utilities etc. Some loans may be secured against your home so these would be treated as priority. You will need to look carefully at your spending and cut down unnecessary expenditure. All of us have to do this, particularly in recession. Look to get cheaper deals on gas and electricity.

Beware that debt management companies, of which there are many, will charge a fee to carry out the planning and negotiating for you. The current economic climate, has provided the perfect opportunity for unscrupulous operators to target vulnerable people. When considering going down the road of a debt management plan you should contact a reputable operator. They should be approved by the Financial Conduct Authority. Advice can be obtained via Citizens Advice or National Debtline (0808 501 6304).

Remember, during the pandemic, there are debt payment holidays in force, such as credit cards and mortgage holidays which should provide some respite.

Structuring a Debt Management Plan

Before you approach a debt management company you will need to collect together information about your financial affairs and follow some simple steps:

- Make a complete list of all your debts-divide them into separate headings such as priority and non-priority debts. You will need to make offers to pay off your priority debts before tackling non-priority debts.

- The next step is to work out your income and expenditure. Be honest and make sure the amounts are realistic. What you are trying to do here is to gain a clear picture of your situation-which can be very beneficial.

- Contact your creditors and inform them that you are putting together a debt management plan.

- Do not borrow extra money to pay off your debts. Think about ways in which you can maximise your income-for example are you claiming all the benefits that you are entitled to.

If you are managing the debt management plan yourself, it is very important that you inform your creditors that you are structuring your debt. They should then be on your side. As debt management plans have no legal standing, creditors do not have to accept them. However, if it comes to court action against you then the fact that you have a plan will stand in your favour. Creditors are not allowed to harass you and if you are being harassed then you should contact an advice agency, such as the Citizens Advice Bureau or National Debtline. It is important, once you have structured your plan, that you let your creditors have a copy so they can see what you are doing and, hopefully, agree to it.

Making payments

Most people will pay their debt management plans by standing order through their bank account. However, it is up to the client of the company how they choose to pay, as long as it is paid in full and on time. If you are thinking of using a debt management company, you should be aware of the following before making your decision:

- Debt management organisations will only be interested in individuals who have some income and can service their debts over time in full-and who own their own home, so that the home can be used as surety against the debts.

- Many debt management organisations will deal only with non-priority debts and leave the individual to deal with priority debts themselves.
- Most debt management companies will charge a fee, typically between £200-250 which leaves less money to pay off the debts. They might also charge a deposit at the outset. However, there are a few companies that will provide the service for free-see below.
- Most debt management companies also charge a fee to the individual each month, an administration fee. This can be quite high. Remember these companies are in business and you are their product.

You need to check the contract that you will have with the company and that you can cancel any time if you are not happy.

Debt management Plans and Credit status

If you are heavily in debt then this is noted on your credit reference file. By entering into a plan with a debt management company, your debts will be cleared based on agreement with creditors. After the agreed payment period is over then your credit status will begin to improve. Negative entries stay on file for six years.

Companies offering a free Debt Management Plan service:
Step change.org 0800 138 1111
Payplan.com 0800 280 2816

****

Chapter 4

Individual Voluntary Arrangements

An Individual Voluntary Arrangement (IVA) is a formal agreement between you and your creditors where you will come to an arrangement with people you owe money to, which will enable you to make reduced payments towards the total amount of your debt in order to pay off a percentage of what you owe then generally after 5 years your debt is classed as settled.

Due to its formal nature, an IVA has to be set up by a licensed professional. You should first go to the official insolvency website: www.gov.uk/government/organisations/insolvency-service or phone the UK Insolvency Helpline for more information (0300 678 0015 Subject to opening during 19) to source a licensed Insolvency Practitioner.

Many firms have jumped on the insolvency bandwagon in the last few years. However, unlike these firms, the Licensed Insolvency Practitioners on the panel do not charge any fees up front for putting together a client's proposals for an Individual Voluntary Arrangement.

How IVA's work

Once a Licensed Insolvency Practitioner has made a decision that an IVA is the correct instrument for you to solve your debt problems, you will then be asked questions regarding your current financial situation. This is an in-depth interview, and, based on the information that you give, a debt repayment plan will be drawn up.

To qualify for an IVA one or more of the following criteria must apply to your situation:

- You must have debts of £12,000 or more although this can vary
- The bulk of your debts must be unsecured
- You must have a regular income
- You are presently employed
- You can supply verification of income

Based on this information, with an assessment of income and outgoings a plan can be drawn up for you. You must scrutinise this plan and then sign it if you agree, or discuss it if you don't.

An application may then be made to court for an interim order. Once this order is in place, no creditors will be able to take legal action against you. Following the grant of this order the Nominee (Licensed Insolvency Practitioner) will circulate to the creditors the following information:

- The Nominee's comments on the debtor's proposals
- The proposals
- Notice of the date and location of the meeting of creditors to vote on the proposals
- A statement of affairs-this effectively being a list of the assets and the liabilities of the debtor
- A schedule advising creditors of the requisite majority required to approve the IVA

- A complete list of creditors. A guide to the fees charged following the approval of the IVA
- A form of proxy for voting purposes
- A creditor meeting will then take place at which you should attend.

For an IVA to be approved, creditors will be called on to vote either for or against the arrangement. If only one creditor votes "for" the IVA, the IVA will be approved. However, if only one creditor votes against the IVA, and they represent less than 25% of your total debt, the meeting will be suspended until a later date, and other creditors who did not vote will be called on to vote.

If the creditor who voted against the IVA represents more than 25% of the total debt you owe then the IVA will fail. This is because an IVA will only ever be approved if 75% in monetary value is voted for. If any of the creditor's don't vote it is assumed that they will vote for the IVA.

The IVA will be legally binding. As long as you keep up the repayments, when the term of your agreement is finished, you will be free from these debts regardless of how much has been paid off. During the period of the arrangement your financial situation will be reviewed regularly to see if there are any changes in your circumstances.

It is worth noting that if you do enter into an IVA with your creditors and have an endowment policy linked to your mortgage, or equity in your property or a pension fund then these will be taken into account when working out income/assets/outgoings.

Key components for a successful IVA

- The IVA must offer a higher return to creditors than could otherwise be expected were the debtor to be made bankrupt.
- An honest declaration of your assets and/or anticipated future earnings should be made. Material or false declarations are very likely to result in an unsuccessful IVA.

Advantages of an IVA-Individual, partner or sole trader

- No restrictions in regards to personal credit although in practice can be hard to obtain.
- The proposals are drawn up by the debtor and are entirely flexible to accommodate personal circumstances.
- The debtor does not suffer the restrictions imposed by bankruptcy, such as not being able to operate as a director of a limited company etc.
- The costs of administering an IVA are considerably lower than in bankruptcy, enabling a higher return to creditors.
- IVA's operate as an insolvency procedure and creditors can as a consequence of this, still reclaim tax and VAT relief as a bad debt.
- Enables a sole trader or partner to continue to trade and generate income towards repayment to creditors.

Disadvantages of an IVA

- Where contributions from income are being made, IVA's are generally expected to be for a period longer than bankruptcy, i.e. 5 years as opposed to 1 year.

- If the debtor fails to comply with the terms of the arrangement his home and assets can still be at risk if they have not been specifically excluded from the proposals.
- If the IVA fails as a consequence of the debtor not meeting obligations, it is likely that the debtor will be made bankrupt at this time.
- There will be no opportunity for a trustee in bankruptcy to investigate the actions of the debtor or possibility of hidden assets.

Companies offering IVA advice

Step Change stepchange.org 0800 138 1111
personaldebtsolutions/IVA 0800 901 2488
National Debt Relief
www.nationaldebtrelief.co.uk 0800 888 6660

****

Chapter 5

Administration Orders

An Administration Order is a single county court order that covers all eligible debts and rolls them up together. A single payment is made every month into the court. The court staff then divides the payment up amongst creditors on a pro-rata basis. Like other court orders, an Administration Order stops creditors from taking further or separate action against you.

Rolling up your eligible debts into an administration order can save you a lot of time and also stress as the court will deal with your debts on your behalf. Any interest and other charges that were being added onto your debts are automatically stopped on the granting of an Administration Order.

There is no initial up-front fee for an Administration Order. The court takes a fee of 10 pence out of every pound owed, which means that the handling fee is 10% of your overall debts. The fee is deducted from payments into court. If you apply for a composition order at the same time that you apply for the Administration Order then the amount of time that you make payments for is limited, usually to three years. This is because, if you are paying only a very small amount to your creditors then the order could go on for years. A Composition Order is a way of making sure that this does not happen. If the judge does decide to make a Composition Order then this is usually limited to three years, meaning that you will have to pay off part of your debts only. If you do not have a Composition Order in place, you can apply for one separately even after your Administration Order is in effect. This can be applied for using form N244.

Who is eligible to apply for an Administration Order?

You can get an Administration order if:

- You have at least two debts.
- Have at least one county court or High Court Judgement against you.
- The total of your debts is less than £5,000.

If you are seeking an Administration Order you can apply on form N92, obtainable online or from your local county court. The form has notes to help you in the completion. The first page of the form will ask you to list all of your debts. It is important that this is completed thoroughly, together with any arrears on priority debts. You should not sign the form at this stage. You need to take it to the county court and sign the declaration in front of a court officer. Always keep a copy of the form.

Once the court has accepted your application, your creditors will be automatically informed that you have applied for an Administration Order. Your creditors then have 16 days in which to lodge any objections that they may have, for example, they may consider that the payments offered are too low. Your creditors can also ask the court to not include them in the Order. Certain creditors, priority creditors, will almost certainly object, such as mortgage, utilities (gas and electricity), as they will want to reach their own arrangements with you.

If no objections are received within 16 days, and the courts are happy with what you have offered, then the Administration Order will be made. The creditors can take no further action provided that you pay what you have offered on time. If there is a problem, then the order should not be refused without a court hearing. A hearing should be arranged at court for you and you should always attend, or write to the court if your reason for non-attendance is valid. Once the order is in place you make your payment to the court and not the creditors.

The Administration Order will last until the debts are paid in full, unless a Composition Order is made. Either the creditors can ask for a review of the order at any time or you can apply to amend it in the light of changing circumstances. Details of the Administration Order are recorded on credit reference files for a period of six years from the date of the order.

Debts

Most courts will expect all of your debts to be listed on the forms, including priority debts such as mortgage. You will need to state whether the debts are in joint names and list them. Joint debts can cause problems as, because there is joint liability the creditors can still go after them. If the other person also has a court order against them and debts of less than £5,000 they can still apply for a separate Administration Order.

One important point to note is that your application may be refused if the information given reveals that you haven't got enough money to pay what you have offered.

Other factors involved in applying for an Administration Order

Certain debts are treated differently to the most common debts. Council tax arrears for previous years can be included in the Administration Order but not the current years bill, unless the council has told you that you have lost the right to pay in instalments and must pay the balance in one lump sum.

Magistrate's court fines can be included in the application but the judge may leave them out. Any social fund loans and benefit overpayments are left out, as they are not ordinary debts.

No longer able to afford payments?

If you find yourself in a position where you can no longer keep up with the terms of the order then you can apply to change the amount that you pay each month. You can use a N244 form and there shouldn't be a fee. You should state that you are applying for a variation of payments you are making under your Administration Order and say why you are applying. You should attach a copy of a personal budget sheet to indicate how you have arrived at the revised figures. The meeting to discuss amendments will be with a District Judge who can make any changes needed. If you don't keep up with the payments in the order then the court can cancel or revoke the Administration Order. If this happens your creditors can then pursue you for the debts.

Administration Order paid off?

When you have paid the Order off in full you can get a Certificate of Satisfaction from the county court. There is a fee for this, currently £15, however check fees as they are subject to change. Details of your Administration Order are kept by the Registry of County Court Judgements and by credit reference agencies. These agencies will mark your file to indicate that the debt has been paid off.

If you have a Composition Order then you can still get a Certificate of Satisfaction to show that the Administration Order has been paid but individual debts will not be marked as satisfied as they have not been paid in full. However, none of the creditors on the Administration Order can take action against you either because it has been paid in full or paid the amount owed under the Composition order.

Companies offering advice on Administration Orders
Debt Advice Foundation debtadvicefoundation.org 0800 043 40 50

National Debtline nationaldebtline.org 0808 808 4000 (provides very useful sample letters to creditors and also an advice pack)

****

Chapter 6

Debt Relief Orders

What is a debt Relief Order?

A debt relief order, which came into force in April 2009, is an order you can apply for if you can't afford to pay off your debts. It is granted by the Insolvency Service and is a cheaper option than going bankrupt. This solution is available in England, Wales and Northern Ireland.

You must have unsecured debts of less than £20,000 and a low income to apply for a debt relief order. It usually lasts for one year and, during that time, none of the people that you owe money to (creditors) will be able to take action against you to get their money back. At the end of the year you will be free of all the debts listed in the order. You can't apply for a debt relief order if you:

- own things of value or have savings of over £1000
- Own a vehicle worth more than £1,000
- Have a private pension fund worth over £300

To apply for a debt relief order, you will need to contact an authorised advisor who will check whether or not you meet the specific conditions and then applies for the order on your behalf. Details of authorised advisors can be obtained from the Insolvency Service, the Law Society or from a Citizens Advice

Bureau. The order will cost you £90 but you can pay this in instalments over six-months.

Who can apply for a debt relief order?

You can only apply for a debt relief order if you meet certain conditions. These are when:

- You have qualifying debts of £20,000 or under. These debts must be of a certain type
- You have disposable income of less than £50 per month after expenses (normal expenses). When you work out this figure you must take into account all of the money that you have coming into your household. This includes salary and wages, any benefits, pension, contributions from other household members and any rental income.
- The assets that you own and any savings are worth less than £1000. Your motor vehicle must be worth less than £1,000 unless it has been specially adapted because you have a physical disability.
- In the last three years you must have lived, had a property or carried on a business in England or Wales.
- You haven't applied for a DRO in the last three years.

Type of debts included in a debt relief order

As explained, only certain types of debts can be included in a debt relief order. These are termed qualifying debts and include:

- Credit cards

- Overdrafts
- Loans
- Rent
- Utilities
- Telephone
- Council tax
- Benefit overpayments
- Social fund loans
- Hire purchase or conditional sale agreements
- Buy now-pay later agreements

Certain types of debts cannot be included such as:
- Court fines and confiscation orders-basically fines relating to criminal activity
- Child support and maintenance
- Student loans

Your assets

Assets are the things of value that you own. As explained above, if you own assets worth more than £1000, or if you have a motor vehicle worth more than £1,000 you won't be able to apply for a debt relief order. Examples of assets that you may own include savings, vehicles, shares, antiques, and property. This is not an exhaustive list. Essentially, anything with a value can be counted as an asset.

In relation to property, if you own a property it is very unlikely that you can apply for a Debt Relief Order. The fact that you may have a mortgage on it will not matter.

If you have not reached retirement age, but have a private or occupational pension fund, then the value of the fund counts towards the £1000 limit. If you have retired and are receiving payments from a pension, then this will be regarded as income rather than an asset.

When working out what is an asset, and the value of an asset, there are some items that you don't have to take into account. These include:

- Household equipment such as bedding clothing and furniture, i.e. essential items.
- Tools, books and any other item of equipment that you may use in your business
- A car which has been specially adapted because you have a physical disability and which you need to carry out your everyday activities.
- A motor vehicle worth less than £1,000.

Those ineligible for a debt relief order

A person cannot get a debt relief order if the following applies:

- Person currently bankrupt
- You have an IVA (Individual Voluntary Arrangement) or are applying for an IVA.
- Creditors have applied to make you bankrupt but the hearing hasn't yet taken place. You might still be able to apply for a debt relief order if your creditors agree.
- You have been given a bankruptcy restrictions order or undertaking.
- You have petitioned for bankruptcy but your petition has not yet been dealt with.

- You have had a Debt Relief Order in the last six years.
- You have been given a debt relief restriction order or undertaking.

Applying for a Debt Relief Order

Debt relief orders are administered by the Official Receiver through the Insolvency Service. However, you can only apply for a debt relief order through a third party or intermediary and not through the Insolvency Service Direct. An intermediary is usually a skilled debt advisor who has been permission to proceed with the advice and paperwork. Intermediaries can be found by going to the Citizens Advice Service website www. Citizensadvice.org.uk.

As mentioned above the cost of applying for a debt relief order is £90, which must be paid in cash at a payzone outlet. A list of these outlets can be found at www.payzone.co.uk. The £90 can be paid in six-monthly instalments. However, the Official receiver won't consider an application until the fee has been paid in full. The fee is non-refundable. It is an offence to give false or misleading statements in your application. Once the debt relief order has been approved then you shouldn't pay any of the creditors listed in the order. Your creditors will be informed about the order and they will be prevented from taking any action. The debt relief order will be published on the Individual Insolvency Register:

www.gov.uk/search-bankruptcy-insolvency-register.
The register is available to the public. Your name and address will remain on the register for 15 months.

Things not to do before applying for a DRO or during the order

There are certain things that you cannot do either before you apply for a DRO or during the life of the DRO. Mainly:

- You cannot hide, destroy or falsify any books or documents up to one year before you apply for an order and during the order period

- You must tell the Official Receiver of any changes in your circumstances that would affect the application between making the application and the order being granted

- You cannot give away or sell things for less than they are worth to help you get a debt relief order.

If you are found guilty of doing any of the above you will be committing an offence which could prevent you obtaining an order or fined or imprisoned. If you have already been granted a debt relief order then the Official Receiver can apply for a Debt Relief Restriction Order or the debt relief order might be taken away.

During the Debt Relief Order period

During the period of a Debt Relief Order you won't have to pay towards the debts listed in the order. The creditors of these debts cannot take any action against you. A Debt Relief Order normally lasts 12 months.

However, as listed above there are certain debts that can't be included in a DRO. These include normal household expenses. You will also have to pay off any debts that are not included in the order. New debts cannot be added once an order is made. You have to tell the Official Receiver about any new debts incurred or if you have forgotten to include any new debts in the order.

Your debt relief order will appear on your credit file and remain on there for six years. This may affect your credit in the future and you might find it difficult to open a bank account. With a Debt Relief Order in place, there are certain things that you cannot do. These are called 'restrictions' and include the following:

- Getting credit over £500 without telling the lender you have a DRO
- Carrying on a business in a different name from the one under which you were given a DRO
- Being involved with promoting, managing or setting up a limited company, without permission from court.

If the Official Receiver believes that you have provided wrong information or have been dishonest they can apply for a Debt Relief Restriction Order. If you are given a Debt Relief Restriction Order, this means that the restrictions on the things that you can do can last from 2-15 years. However, the DRO will still end 12 months after being granted and you won't have to pay off any debts listed in the order. If you don't follow the restrictions you will be committing an offence.

Changes in circumstances
You have the responsibility to inform the Official Receiver of any changes in your circumstances during the period of the DRO. This includes any assets of real value that you acquire during the DRO, e.g. money that has been left you. Failure to inform the

Official Receiver might mean the cancelling of your DRO and you will then be responsible for all debts listed in the DRO.

****

PART 3

THE PROCESS OF BANKRUPTCY

ENGLAND AND WALES

Chapter 7

The Process of Bankruptcy-England and Wales

Bankruptcy is one way of dealing with debts that you can no longer pay. The bankruptcy proceedings free you from debts which have simply become overwhelming and enable you to make a fresh start, subject to some restrictions outlined later. The process of bankruptcy also makes sure that your assets are shared out fairly between your creditors.

If you have decided that any of the alternatives to bankruptcy outlined in the previous chapters are not for you, and that bankruptcy is your only option, you need to be clear about the process of bankruptcy and what this entails and also the impact that it will have on the next few years following bankruptcy.

As well as applying for bankruptcy yourself, someone else you owe money to (a creditor) can apply to make you bankrupt, even if you don't want them to. For a creditor to make you bankrupt, you must owe at least £5,000. However, in order to put yourself in a more favourable position, you can always apply for a Fast Track Voluntary Arrangement.

Fast-Track Voluntary Arrangement (FTVA)
FTVA's were introduced by the Enterprise Act 2002. If you have been made bankrupt by one of your creditors but think that you can provide a significantly better return to your creditors than they will receive through your bankruptcy, then by entering into a Fast Track Voluntary Arrangement (FTVA) you can get your

bankruptcy annulled. An FTVA is a binding agreement made between you and your creditors to pay all or part of the money you owe. It can only be entered into after you have been made bankrupt. In order to enter into a FTVA you must secure the co-operation of the Official Receiver, who will act as your nominee. They will help you put together your proposal for your creditors.

For the FTVA to be accepted, 75% of the creditors who vote must agree to the proposal. It is then legally binding, and no creditor can take legal action regarding the debt provided you keep to the agreement. As nominee, the Official Receiver will then supervise the arrangement, making payment to your creditors in accordance with your proposals.

Costs of the FTVA

The fee for acting as nominee is £300 at 2020. However, this should be checked. Additionally, for carrying out the ongoing role of supervisor of the FTVA the Official Receiver will charge fifteen per cent of monies from any assets you own or any money collected from you. You will also be required to pay a £15 registration fee for your FTVA to be recorded on the public register of individual voluntary arrangements.

Duration of the FTVA

There is no fixed period for a FTVA. It lasts as long as is agreed and will be outline in the proposal. Once the FTVA has been agreed the Official Receiver will apply to have your bankruptcy annulled, as if it never existed. You will no longer be subject to the restrictions in the bankruptcy order. However, if you fail to comply with the order then the Official Receiver will make you bankrupt again. If the circumstances are beyond your control, such as being made redundant then the Official Receiver will take no action against you. However, your creditors can once again petition for your bankruptcy.

Bankruptcy

Advantages of going bankrupt

There are a number of advantages to going bankrupt. When the bankruptcy order is over you can make a fresh start - in many cases this can be after a year. Other advantages of going bankrupt include:

- the pressure is taken off you because you don't have to deal with your creditors and you're allowed to keep certain things, like household goods and a reasonable amount to live on
- creditors have to stop most types of court action to get their money back following a bankruptcy order
- the money you owe can (usually) be written off

Disadvantages of going bankrupt

There are disadvantages of going bankrupt which include:
- if your income is high enough, you'll be asked to make payments towards your debts for 3 years
- it will be more difficult to take out credit while you're bankrupt and your credit rating will be affected for 6 years
- if you own your home, it might have to be sold and some of your possessions might have to be sold, for example, your car and any luxury items you own

- if you are, or are about to be, the right age to get your pension savings, these might be affected (see below)
- some professions don't let people who have been made bankrupt carry on working
- if you own a business it might be closed down and the assets sold off
- going bankrupt can affect your immigration status
- your bankruptcy will be published publicly (although if you're worried you or your family maybe the victims of violence, you can ask that your details aren't given out). You can get a Person At Risk of Violence Order (PARV)

PARV order

When you're made bankrupt, your name and address will be published in:

- the Individual Insolvency Register
- the London Gazette

If having your address published will put you at risk of violence, you can apply to the court for a person at risk of violence (PARV) order. Your name will still be published, but your address won't be.

You can only apply for a PARV if you've already started a bankruptcy application.

How to apply

Download and fill in application form 7.1A from the Insolvency Service website.

Take your completed form to your nearest court that deals with bankruptcy. They'll tell you if you need to pay a fee to apply. You'll have to go to a hearing to present your application to a judge - the court will tell you when and where this will take place. You'll usually get a decision on the same day.

Submit your bankruptcy application once you have your PARV order.

Debts that bankruptcy covers

Becoming bankrupt means that many of your debts will be written off. However, it is important to understand that bankruptcy doesn't cover all debts

Which debts are included in bankruptcy?

Most debts that you have when a bankruptcy order is made will be covered by your bankruptcy. This means they will automatically be written off at the end of the bankruptcy period. However, not all types of debt are written off. The people you owe these debts to can still take action to get their money back. This means that before you apply for bankruptcy you should work out how you'll deal with any debts that aren't covered.

Debts that aren't automatically written off include the following:

- magistrates court fines
- any payments a court has ordered you to make under a confiscation order, for example, for drug trafficking
- maintenance payments and child support payments, including any lump sum orders and costs that have arisen from family proceedings, although you may be able to

ask the court to order that you don't have to pay this debt
- student loans
- secured loans and other secured debts, such as debts secured with a charging order
- debts you owe because of the personal injury or death of another person, although you may be able to ask the court to order that you don't have to pay this debt
- social fund loans
- some benefits and tax credits overpayments.

Mortgages and bankruptcy

Bankruptcy won't stop your mortgage lender from taking steps to repossess your home if you're behind on your mortgage. However, if your home is repossessed and sold, but doesn't raise enough money to pay off your outstanding mortgage or any other debt secured on it, the remaining debt will no longer be secured. This means you'll be released from it at the end of your bankruptcy. You'll also be released from it even if your home is sold at any time after your bankruptcy has ended.

Debts you took out by fraud

If you took out any of your debts by fraud, your creditor can't chase you to pay while you're bankrupt, but they won't be written off at the end of the bankruptcy period. This means you'll still be liable for paying debts you obtained by fraud after you've been discharged from bankruptcy.

*

Debts in joint names

If you owe debts jointly with someone else, you can include these in your bankruptcy. However, the creditor would then be able to chase the other person for the whole of the amount that is owed. In practice, this only happens when the other person is working. You and the other person can each apply for bankruptcy individually, which would cover the joint debt. You will each need to pay a fee and a deposit separately. You can't jointly apply for bankruptcy.

Business debts

If you have business debts that were taken out in a partnership, you can make a joint application for bankruptcy as long as all the partners agree. If you're thinking about doing this, you should take specialist advice.

More information

Dealing with debt - how to wind up a partnership' from the Insolvency Service at www.bis.gov.uk

Business Debtline (BDL) is a charity which offers free, impartial and confidential advice to businesses in financial difficulty in the UK both on its website and by a helpline. Business Debtline-Freephone: 0800 197 6026 (Monday to Friday from 9am to 5pm) Website: www.bdl.org.uk

How to go bankrupt

It is expensive to go bankrupt although not as expensive as before now that the process is online. You can apply to go bankrupt online by filling in a form at gov.uk/apply-for-bankruptcy. It will cost £680. You won't get this money back if a bankruptcy order is made. You can either pay:

- online - you can pay the fee in instalments this way
- by cash at any Royal Bank of Scotland branch - you can't pay in instalments this way

If you make false statements on the form, or don't tell the truth about all your property, this is a criminal offence. If you need help filling in the form, contact the Insolvency Service enquiry line:

Insolvency Service enquiry line
Telephone: 0300 678 0015
Open Monday to Friday, 8am to 5pm (check website)

Email: insolvency.enquiryline@insolvency.gsi.gov.uk

You can also contact an advice agency such as Citizens Advice or the National Debtline on 0808 808 4000.

If your application is accepted and a bankruptcy order is made, your money will come under the control of the Official Receiver. The Official Receiver will arrange an interview with you. After your interview, they will tell your creditors about the bankruptcy and send them a report with a summary of your financial situation. Your assets may be sold to pay off some or all of your debts.

Your name and bankruptcy details will be published on the national register of bankruptcies, called the Individual Insolvency

Register. As we have seen, you can apply for a PARV (Person at Risk of Violence) Order if you fear for your safety in any way.

Dealing with the official receiver after bankruptcy

When you become bankrupt, the official receiver will take control of all your property. You will need to provide them with certain information about your finances and you have a duty to co-operate with them.

What the official receiver does

The official receiver's role in your bankruptcy includes the following:

- taking control of some of your property
- assessing whether you can afford to make any payments towards your debts
- investigating your conduct and financial affairs before and during the bankruptcy, which may include asking you to attend an interview, complete a questionnaire or attend a public examination
- advertising your bankruptcy in the London Gazette
- informing your creditors of your bankruptcy, which may include arranging a meeting of all the creditors that you must attend
- in some cases, acting as the trustee of your bankruptcy, responsible for distributing your property and money between your creditors.

The official receiver will usually be told about your bankruptcy order on the day that it's made. You'll then hear from the official receiver within two working days.

The official receiver may send you a questionnaire asking for full details of your financial situation. You will need to fill in and return the questionnaire within the timescale you're given, and get together all the records you have about your property and financial situation.

Interview

You'll be given an appointment for an interview (check current COVID situation) with the official receiver, which must take place within ten working days of your bankruptcy order being made. The interview will usually take place over the telephone. During the interview, the official receiver will:

- check the information in your questionnaire, if you were asked to complete one
- ask for any other information about your property and debts that is needed, along with questions about the situation that led to your bankruptcy
- deal with any queries you may have about how the bankruptcy will work or your own particular case.

The interview may last anywhere from half an hour to three hours, depending on how simple or complicated your case is.

Public examination

The official receiver can require you to appear at a public examination, if at least half your creditors ask for this. At the examination you have to declare an oath in open court on the details of your financial situation. If you don't attend you may be arrested and could be fined or, in very limited circumstances, sent to prison.

Creditors' meeting

The official receiver may arrange a meeting of all your creditors. If this happens, you may be required to attend. At the meeting, the creditors may appoint an insolvency practitioner as the trustee of your bankruptcy, who would be responsible for raising cash from your property and belongings.

Income payments agreement

One of the aims of bankruptcy is that creditors should receive at least part payment of what they are owed, if possible. This means that if your income is high enough, you can be asked to make contributions towards your bankruptcy debts under an income payments agreement (IPA). If you don't agree to this, the court could make an income payments order (IPO). An IPA:

- is a formal, legally binding agreement between you and the bankruptcy trustee
- means you'll usually make regular monthly payments towards your debts, although you could also be asked to make a one-off lump sum payment
- normally lasts for three years, even though you will usually be discharged from bankruptcy earlier than this
- is normally a minimum of £20 per month
- doesn't require you to go to court
- can be changed if your financial circumstances change.

If your only income is from benefits, you won't be asked to make an IPA. If you have any income that isn't from benefits, such as wages or maintenance, you'll only be asked to make an IPA if you're bankrupt and you have more than £20 of disposable income each month after paying for you and your family's bills and day-to-day living expenses.

If you have more than £20 of disposable income each month but don't agree to the IPA, the bankruptcy trustee can apply to the courts for an income payments order (IPO). This would mean a proportion of your salary or wages would be paid to the trustee. You'll be given at least 28 days' notice of the court hearing. You can either:

- agree to the IPO, which would mean there won't be a court hearing
- oppose the IPO, meaning you'd have to attend the court hearing and explain why you oppose it.

Your disposable income is what's left after the reasonable day-to-day living expenses for you and your family have been paid. The official receiver will always consider your views about what is 'reasonable' or necessary spending for your circumstances, but these expenses would normally include:

- your rent or mortgage payments
- food
- heating and lighting
- TV licence
- broadband and telephone service
- household insurance

- car tax and insurance, if the trustee has allowed you to keep your car
- membership of the AA, RAC or similar, if you're allowed to keep your car
- professional membership fees that are part of your job and not paid by your employer
- prescriptions, dental treatment and opticians' fees
- payments under a maintenance order or child support agency assessment
- a reasonable monthly cost of a mobile phone
- dry cleaning.

Reasonable amounts of spending on other items may also be considered, including:

- clothing
- holidays
- hairdressers
- extra-curricular activities for your children
- after-school clubs
- pets.

The following spending would not generally be classed as reasonable day-to-day living expenses, although there may be situations where you can argue otherwise:

- gym membership, sports expenses or club membership, although you may be able to argue you need this for medical purposes

- pension contributions you're making to enhance a private pension
- private health insurance
- money for gambling, alcohol or cigarettes
- satellite TV, although if you have a 'combined' package with broadband and telephone service, the official receiver will look at whether this saves money overall
- excessive mortgage payments
- regular payments to charities or religious organisations.
- If your circumstances change

If you're paying an IPA or IPO and your circumstances change, you should tell the trustee straight away. A change of circumstances could include your income has gone up or down, you've received a lump sum payment, for example through an inheritance or you're having financial difficulties, such as losing your job. The trustee will look at the change in your circumstances and decide whether your IPA or IPO needs to be changed. Depending on the change in your circumstances, the IPA or IPO could be suspended, payments could be increased or you could be asked to pay a proportion of lump sum towards it. If the trustee won't agree to change the amount, you could ask the court to order that it is changed.

Bankruptcy restrictions orders
Before you're discharged from bankruptcy you have to follow certain rules, covering things like getting credit and your working life. These are called restrictions. If the official receiver finds out you've behaved dishonestly or recklessly, a bankruptcy

restrictions order (BRO) may be made against you. This would extend the period of restrictions for anything up to 15 years.

What is a BRO?

A BRO is a legal order from the court which extends the period of time for which you have to follow certain restrictions. As stated, this can be for anything from two to 15 years. The restrictions are the same as the ones you have to follow during the year before you're discharged from bankruptcy, which say you can't do any of the following:

- get credit of £500 or more without telling the lender that you have a BRO
- act as a director or get involved with setting up, promoting or running a company without permission from the court
- carry out a business in a different name from the one under which you were made bankrupt, without telling everyone you do business with the name in which you were made bankrupt
- act as an insolvency practitioner.

Extra restrictions

With a BRO, you also have to follow some extra restrictions. For example, you can't:

- act as a local councillor
- be a school governor
- hold certain other positions in associations, governing bodies or professions
- exercise any 'right to buy'
- be a Member of Parliament in England or Wales.

Other consequences of a BRO

As well as the restrictions a BRO places upon you, there are other consequences for you if a BRO is made. These include:

- your creditors will be told about the BRO
- the court will issue a press notice about your BRO, which the local newspapers and media can publish if they wish to
- your details will appear on the publicly available insolvency register, which any member of the public can view
- details of your BRO may also be published on the Insolvency Services Restrictions Outcomes webpage.

Getting a bankruptcy cancelled

In some situations you can apply to cancel your bankruptcy. You have to do this by applying to the court where you were originally made bankrupt. The cancellation of bankruptcy is called annulment and legally puts you back into the same position as you would be if the bankruptcy order had never been made.

When can bankruptcy be cancelled?

You can apply to have your bankruptcy cancelled for any of the following reasons:

- you've paid your bankruptcy debts and the bankruptcy expenses in full or have made arrangements to secure or guarantee them, for example against property that you own

- if you were made bankrupt by one or more of your creditors but you think the bankruptcy order should never have been made, for example, because you owed less than £5000 or you had a different defence to the making of a bankruptcy order
- your creditors have approved an individual voluntary arrangement (IVA).

Effects of cancelling bankruptcy

The cancellation of bankruptcy puts you back into the same position legally as if the bankruptcy order was never made. However, there are some things that can't be reversed and you may also need to take action yourself to get some records changed. The main things to be aware of are:

- you'll become liable for paying any of your debts that haven't yet been paid in the bankruptcy
- you'll lose any property that the official receiver or trustee has already sold or disposed of
- any property or belongings that haven't yet been disposed of will be given back to you
- the record of your bankruptcy will be removed from the Insolvency Register five days after the cancellation
- if a bankruptcy notice has been registered against a property you own, you can apply to the Land Registry to have the notice removed

it's your responsibility to tell credit reference agencies about the cancellation of your bankruptcy, so that they can update their records and your credit reference file.

How you apply to cancel bankruptcy

If you want to cancel your bankruptcy, the process you should follow depends on the reason why you want it to be annulled.

If you've paid your debts and expenses in full

To apply for annulment because you've paid your bankruptcy debts and expenses in full, you should follow this process:

- complete an application form, called Form 7.1a, which you can get from the court or from the Insolvency Service
- make a written witness statement, setting out the details of your debts and the bankruptcy expense. Give details of payments you've made and proof of these
- return the application form and witness statement to the court, which will then set a date for a hearing
- tell the official receiver or bankruptcy trustee about the hearing at least 28 days in advance, and send them a copy of your application and witness statement
- the trustee will send a report to the court to confirm whether you've paid your debts and explain how you've conducted your financial affairs during the bankruptcy
- attend the court hearing.

You'll need to pay an application fee, but depending on your circumstances, you may be able to get this waived or reduced.

If the bankruptcy order shouldn't have been made

To apply for annulment because you think the bankruptcy order shouldn't have been made, you should follow this process:

- complete an application form, called Form 7.1a, which you can get from the court or from the Insolvency Service at www.bis.gov.uk/insolvency
- make a written witness statement, saying why the bankruptcy order should not have been made
- return the application form and witness statement to the court, which will then set a date for a hearing
- notify the official receiver or bankruptcy trustee of the hearing and send them a copy of your application and witness statement
- attend the court hearing.

You'll need to pay an application fee, but depending on your circumstances, you may be able to get this waived or reduced. Even if the bankruptcy is cancelled, you may still have to pay for the costs of the bankruptcy order and the annulment hearing. The court will decide who should pay these costs when it hears the case.

If your bankruptcy order is cancelled because it shouldn't have been made, any bankruptcy restrictions orders or bankruptcy restrictions undertakings that have been made against you will also be cancelled.

If your creditors have agreed an IVA

If your creditors have agreed your proposal for an individual voluntary arrangement (IVA), either you or the supervisor of the IVA must apply to the court for your bankruptcy to be cancelled. This can only be done 28 days after the creditors have agreed to your proposal. You can apply using the same procedure as an application where the bankruptcy order shouldn't have been made.

Generally:

Accessing your bank account after going bankrupt

When you're declared bankrupt, your bank account may be frozen immediately. You may not be able to use it again and might find you have problems getting another bank account. Some banks may let you keep using your existing bank account, but this might only happen after they've frozen it for some time while they speak to the official receiver. If you want to keep using your existing bank account, you should ask your bank whether this is possible. Bear in mind that they don't have to say yes, and that the official receiver doesn't have any influence over their decision.

Opening a new bank account

You can open a new bank or building society account after being declared bankrupt, but you the bank or building society may ask if you are bankrupt. They will decide whether or not you can open a new account. Even if the bank agrees to you opening an account, it may impose certain conditions or limits, such as not giving you access to an overdraft.

If you've been refused a bank account

You may find that no bank will agree to you opening an account with them. If this applies to you, you have three main options:

- apply for a basic bank account
- open a Post Office card account
- get a prepaid debit card.

The best solution for you will depend on what kind of income you have and the kinds of payments you want to make.

Basic bank accounts

Basic bank accounts are very simple, so they don't provide a cheque book or overdraft. You can:

- have wages, salary, benefits, pensions and tax credits paid straight into your account
- pay cheques in for free (as long as they're not in foreign currency)
- get money out at Post Offices and cash machines
- pay your bills by direct debit or standing order, and
- use bank counters to pay money in, take it out or check your account balance.

Post Office card account

A Post Office card account may be suitable for you if your income is made up of the following only:

- benefit payments
- state pensions
- tax credit payments.

You can't use this account to receive any other payments, including:

- housing benefit
- payments from a workplace pension
- wages or salary.

This account may suit you if you want a simple account that won't let you go overdrawn. Your credit record won't be checked when you open this account.

Prepaid debit card

Prepaid debit cards give you a way to deal with making payments to other people. They can be used in the same way that an ordinary debit or credit card can be used. This includes:

- paying bills
- transferring money
- taking money out of an ATM.

With a prepaid card you're limited to spending only the amount of money that you put on the card. You can normally 'top up' the cards with cash at a Post Office or Paypoint machine. Many prepaid cards charge a fee for different kinds of transactions, so bear this in mind when you're deciding whether to get one.

Your home

If you own your home, whether freehold or leasehold, solely or jointly, mortgaged or other wise, your interest in the home will form part of your estate which will be dealt with by the trustee. The home may have to be sold to go towards paying your debts. If your spouse and/or children are living with you, it may be possible for the sale of the property to be put off until after the end of the first year of your bankruptcy. This gives time for other housing arrangements to be made.

Your husband, wife/partner, relative or friend may be able to buy your interest in your home from the trustee. If the trustee cannot, for the time being, sell your property he or she may obtain a charging order on your interest in it, but only if that interest is worth more than £1,000. If a charging order is obtained, your interest in the property will be returned to you, but the legal charge over your interest will remain. The amount covered by the legal charge will be the total value of your interest in the property and this sum must be paid from your share of the proceeds when you sell the property.

Until your interest in the property is sold, or until the trustee obtains a charging order over it, that interest will continue to belong to the trustee but only for a certain period, usually only 3 years, and will include any increase in its value. The benefit of any increase in value will go to the trustee to pay debts, even if the home is sold some time after you have been discharged from bankruptcy.

Pension rights

A trustee cannot claim a pension as an asset if your bankruptcy petition was presented on or after May 29th 2000, as long as the pension scheme has been approved by HM Revenue and Customs. For petitions presented before May 29th 2000, trustees can claim some kind of pensions. Generally, the trustee will be able to claim any interest that you have in a life assurance policy.

The trustee may be entitled to sell or surrender the policy and collect any proceeds on behalf of your creditors. If the policy is held in joint names, for instance with your husband or wife, that other person is likely to have an interest in the policy and should contact the trustee immediately to discuss how their interest in the policy should be dealt with.

Your life insurance policy

You may want a life insurance policy to be kept going. You should ask the trustee about this. It may be possible for your interest to be transferred for an amount equivalent to the present value of that interest.

If the life insurance policy has been legally charged to any person, for instance an endowment policy used as security for your mortgage, the rights of the secured creditor will not be affected by the making of the bankruptcy order. But any remaining value in the policy may belong to the trustee.

Your wages

Your trustee may apply to court for an Income Payments Order (IPO) which requires you to make contributions towards the bankruptcy debts from your income. The court will not make an IPO if it would leave you without enough income to meet the reasonable needs of you and your family. The IPO can be increased or decreased to reflect any changes in income.

IPO payments continue for a maximum of 3 years from the date of the order and may continue after you have been discharged from bankruptcy. Or you may enter into a written agreement with your trustee, called an Income Payments Agreement (IPA), to pay a certain amount of your income to the trustee for an agreed period, which cannot be longer than 3 years. Each case is assessed individually.

Restrictions on a bankrupt

The following are criminal offences for an un-discharged bankrupt:

- Obtaining credit of £500 or more either alone or jointly with any other person without disclosing your bankruptcy. This is not just borrowed money but any kind of credit whatsoever.
- Carrying on business (directly or indirectly) in a different name from that in which you were made bankrupt, without telling all of those with whom you are doing business the name in which you were made bankrupt.
- Being concerned (directly or indirectly) in promoting, forming or managing a limited company, or acting as a company director, without the court's permission, whether formally appointed as a director or not.

You may not hold certain public offices. You may not hold office as a trustee of a charity or a pension fund. After the bankruptcy order, you may open a new bank account but you should tell them that you are bankrupt. They may impose conditions and limitations. You should ensure that you do not obtain overdraft facilities without informing the bank that you are bankrupt, or write cheques that are likely to be dishonoured.

Ending bankruptcy

If you were made bankrupt on or after April 1st 2004, you will automatically be freed from bankruptcy after a maximum of twelve months. This period may be shorter if the Official receiver concludes his enquiries into your affairs and files a notice in court. You will also become free from bankruptcy immediately if the court cancels the bankruptcy order. This would normally happen when your debts and fees and expenses of the bankruptcy proceedings have been paid in full, or the bankruptcy order should not have been made. On the other hand, if you have not carried out your duties under the bankruptcy proceedings, the Official Receiver or your trustee may apply to the court for the discharge to be postponed. If the court agrees, your bankruptcy will only end when the suspension has been lifted and the time remaining on your bankruptcy period has run.

Debts

Discharge releases you from most of the debts you owed at the date of the bankruptcy order. Exceptions include debts arising from fraud and any claims which cannot be made in the bankruptcy itself. You will only be released from a liability to pay damages for personal injuries to any person if the court see fit. When you are discharged you can borrow money and carry on business without these restrictions. You can act as a company director, unless disqualified.

Assets that you obtained or owned before your discharge

When you are discharged there may still be assets that you owned, either when your bankruptcy began, or which you obtained before your discharge, which the trustee has not yet dealt with. Examples of these may be an interest in your home, an assurance policy or an inheritance. These assets are still controlled by the trustee who can deal with them at any time in the future. This may not be for a number of years after your discharge.

Assets you obtain after your discharge

Usually, you may keep all assets after your discharge.

Debts incurred after you have been made bankrupt

Bankruptcy deals with your debts at the time of the bankruptcy order. After that date you should manage your finances a lot more carefully. New debts can result in a further bankruptcy order or prosecution.

Credit reference agencies

After you have been discharged from bankruptcy, you will want to ensure that you have a clear idea of your credit rating and also that the details that the credit agencies hold on you is correct. The three main consumer credit reference agencies in the UK are Experian, Equifax and Call Credit. They provide lenders with information about potential borrowers which in turn enables the lenders to make their decisions. The agencies hold information about most adults in the UK. However, sometimes this information is out of date, or incorrect in other ways which can adversely affect your credit.

If personal information about you is incorrect or out of date you have the right to change it under the Data Protection Act 2018. You can ask for a copy of your credit report inline or by post from a credit reference agency for £2. You need to provide your name, and any previous name such as maiden name, address and any addresses lived in for the last six years and your date of birth. The credit reference agency must provide you with details within seven working days. The contact details of the main agencies are as follows:

Experian www.experian.co.uk
Equifax www.equifax.co.uk
Call Credit www.callcredit.co.uk

In addition, there are numerous other agencies which can be accessed on the web, some of them free.

Checking the information on your credit file

A bankruptcy will stay on your credit file for six years from the date of your bankruptcy order. You should ensure that the date of your discharge from bankruptcy is correctly shown. If it is not, you should send your certificate of discharge to the agency as proof. Alternatively, a letter of discharge can be obtained from the Official receiver. Accounts included in your bankruptcy order may show on your credit report as being in default. The date of the default should be no later than the bankruptcy order.

Making a complaint

If the credit reference agency still does not amend the problem after you have contacted them then you can write to the Information Commissioner, who has responsibility for enforcing the Data Protection Act. You should write giving all details of yourself and the problem and they will decide on the action to take. The Information Commissioners Office can be contacted on 0303 123 1133. Website www.ico.gov.uk

You can, if you so wish use credit repair companies who will, for a fee, undertake checking and rectification of your credit rating.

****

PART 4

SCOTLAND AND NORTHERN IRELAND- BANKRUPTCY AND ALTERNATIVES TO BANKRUPTCY

Chapter 8

Bankruptcy and Alternatives to Bankruptcy in Scotland

Scotland's Insolvency Service is called the Accountancy in Bankruptcy www.aib.gov.uk/about-aib/contact-us.

Coronavirus - more protection from action by creditors

If you're worried about creditors taking enforcement action against you or you are thinking of applying for Bankruptcy (sequestration), a Protected Trust Deed or the Debt Arrangement Scheme (DAS) you can apply for a moratorium, which prevents creditors taking action whilst you seek advice. The moratorium protects you for six months but it does not stop interest or charges building and may impact on your credit rating.

If you are worried remember that creditors and sheriff officers should be reacting sympathetically to Covid 19 related financial hardship and you should ask them to treat you fairly as per the Financial Conduct Authority's rules. If this does not work and your creditor has sent you a document called a "Charge for Payment for Money" giving you 14 days to pay your debt in full, then you should apply for a moratorium.

You can apply for a moratorium yourself but it is recommended you only do this after getting advice. Once you have applied for a moratorium bear in mind that if you do not get advice within 6 months, and make an application for either DAS, protected trust deed or bankruptcy, then it will expire and your creditors can take action again.

Changes to Bankruptcy rules in Scotland

Last year, temporary changes to the bankruptcy process were brought in by the Scottish government, to help individuals financially impacted by the pandemic. Scottish ministers have now introduced the *Bankruptcy (Miscellaneous amendments) (Scotland) Regulations 2021*, to make some of those changes permanent.

The main purpose of these measures is to improve access to minimal asset process bankruptcy ("MAP" a form of bankruptcy typically aimed at people with low income and few assets) and to reduce the cost for debtors seeking bankruptcy more widely.

From 29 March 2021, the following key changes came into force:

- The limit for a person to enter a minimal asset process bankruptcy will be permanently increased from £17,000 to £25,000. The fee payable will remain at the reduced sum of £50.

- The fee for accessing an ordinary bankruptcy (also known as 'full administration') will be remain at the reduced cost of £150.

- Anyone in receipt of relevant benefits will be permanently exempted from having to pay a fee if they are seeking MAP or full administration bankruptcy.

- Electronic signature of most MAP and full administration bankruptcy forms will remain a permanent feature, allowing legal paperwork to be completed from home.

The Scottish government has described the improvements as a sensible step in response to the immediate economic impact of the pandemic, but also for the longer term.

In recent years, it could be said that the Scottish government has moved personal insolvency in a generally more debtor friendly direction and the increase of the MAP threshold together with the reduction in fees for debtors seeking bankruptcy appears consistent with that approach. These changes are small but significant alterations to bankruptcy law in Scotland, which could offer easier access to debt to individuals who are experiencing serious financial issues.

It remains to be seen whether any of the other temporary changes introduced, such as the increase in the minimum amount of debt required for a creditor petition to take place - will be extended or made permanent.

Sequestration in Scotland

Taking into account the above, to be eligible for Sequestration (bankruptcy) in Scotland you have to meet certain criteria. You must:

- Have lived in Scotland for 1 day, although extra evidence may be requested to prove that you intend to stay in the country
- Owe more than £3,000
- Not have been sequestrated in the last five years and earlier

- Be classed as apparently insolvent, which could mean a creditor has issued a statutory demand or a charge for payment, or:
- You were not able to get your Trust Deed protected (by signing the paperwork for this you have declared yourself insolvent), or;
- Obtained a Certificate of Sequestration

You can get a Certificate For Sequestration from an Insolvency Practitioner once they have looked over your finances and deemed you can no longer pay your creditors and request sequestration. A Money Advisor is also able to issue you with a Certificate Of Sequestration but only if they are on the government list of approved advisors.

Once you have your certificate, then within 30 days you simply apply for your sequestration to the Accountant in bankruptcy (AIB).There is a £150 fee for applying for sequestration. In some cases this can be zero, depending on what benefits you might be on.

If your application is submitted with the correct evidence and your fee, the AIB will try to process the application within 5 working days, so you could be declared formally bankrupt within 5 working days of them receiving your application and a Trustee will be appointed over your affairs.

At this point the Trustee who may be an Insolvency Practitioner or the Accountants In Bankruptcy, assesses your assets to see if any can be sold to release some cash to your creditors, and also assesses your income and expenditure to see if you can afford to make any payment to your creditors. The Account In Bankruptcy is what is known as the default Trustee, which means if you don't want to go and find an IP yourself to act as Trustee they are appointed to deal with your affairs.

Within 60 days of you being sequestrated, all of your creditors will be told by your IP about your sequestration, however from the date of your order you will never have to deal with them again. They may ring or write to you, but all you do is pass them over to your IP. You don't have to tell them anything and don't have to get drawn in to any conversations with them. It can take time for creditors to react to notices from your IP, especially if your debt is being pursued by agents or other organisations but eventually your IP will take care of all the creditors and ensure that you are in a position so you can start again.

Twelve months from the date you were granted your Award of Bankruptcy you will should be discharged from the arrangement. If you need a certificate to show that you have been discharged, you can apply to the Accountant In Bankruptcy on payment of a small fee (£11 at the time of writing but subject to temporary suspension of fees). However, that doesn't mean the work of your Trustee is complete – depending how complex your case is, their work may continue in the background. You will have to cooperate with your Trustee and you may receive a letter from your Trustee keeping you up to date with what is happening, but you are free to begin to rebuild your life and your credit rating as soon as possible.

If you are able to afford them, you will be required to make payments towards your debts from your income for 36 months. Although you are discharged from bankruptcy after 12 months you will continue to make your payments as long as you can afford them until the 36 months are completed.

Alternatives to Sequestration

Minimal asset process (MAP) bankruptcy

A Minimal Asset Process (MAP) bankruptcy, which came into effect in Scotland on 1st April 2015, and replaced the previous Low-Income Low- Asset Test gives you a fresh start by writing off debts that you can't repay within a reasonable time. It's aimed at people with a low income and not many assets, and is cheaper and more straightforward than sequestration bankruptcy.

This solution is only available to people living in Scotland. If you live in England, Wales or Northern Ireland you may be able to apply for a debt relief order, which is a similar solution, but it's important to note that it has different benefits, risks and fees associated with it.

Who can apply for MAP bankruptcy?

To apply you must meet the following conditions:

- You live in Scotland
- You're on a low income. This can be defined in two ways: Your income is made up solely of income-related benefits such as jobseekers allowance (JSA), or the amount of money you earn covers your essential living costs but you have nothing left over
- Your debts are more than £1,500 and less than £25,000 Your car is worth £3,000 or less
- Your other assets are worth less than £2,000 in total, with no single item worth more than £1,000
- You're not a homeowner , must not own land
- You haven't been bankrupt in the last five years

There are certain debts that cannot be included in MAP sequestration.

These include:
Student loans
Court fines
Arrears of Child Maintenance payments

How MAP bankruptcy works
To apply for MAP you need to pay a fee of £50. This fee may be reduced to NIL if you are on certain benefits. You'll also need to get advice from an approved money advice organisation such as Scotland Debt Solutions www.scotlanddebt.co.uk. You can't apply without doing this.

You should also be aware that with MAP bankruptcy your details will be added to a public register, called the Register of Insolvencies (ROI), for a period of five years.

It will normally last for six months. At this point, your debts are written off, but you can't apply for any further credit for six months. Most debts are included, but if you have any court fines, student loans or child maintenance arrears, you'll need to keep paying these as normal.

Trust deeds
What is a trust deed?
A trust deed is a less formal procedure for personal insolvency in Scotland. It is a contract signed by a debtor by which he or she conveys his or her estate to a licensed IP who is appointed Trustee to realise the debtor's assets for the benefit of creditors.

Trust Deeds become protected trust deeds provided specific level of objections are not received by the trustee within a specified period.

Protected Trust Deed

A protected trust deed is one that is binding on all creditors. The total amount of the debtor's debts (including interest) at the date on which the trust deed is granted must be £3,000 or more. Provided the debtor complies with the terms of their protected trust deed, the creditors can take no further action to pursue the debt or to make the debtor bankrupt.

A protected trust deed prevents the debtor from applying for their own bankruptcy or for a debt payment programme under the Debt Arrangement Scheme.

If a debtor acquires any new debts after they sign the trust deed, they will not be protected from action by their new creditors.

Voluntary Trust Deed

A trust deed is a voluntary agreement between a debtor and their creditors (the people they owe money to) to repay part of what they owe. A trust deed transfers the debtor's rights to the things that they own to a trustee who will sell them to pay creditors part of what is owed to them. A trust deed will normally include a contribution from income for a specified period, this is a minimum of 48 months but can vary. A trustee may determine a shorter payment period where the full amount of the debtor's debt (including interest) at the date on which the trust deed is granted is met. The trustee must be a qualified insolvency practitioner. Insolvency practitioners are regulated by law and must be members of an approved governing body. Independent Insolvency Practitioners' fees are at their own discretion.

An ordinary trust deed is not binding on creditors unless they agree to its terms.

Benefits of a Trust Deed

Certain trust deeds may be registered as "protected", thereby preventing creditors from petitioning for the debtor's sequestration. The main advantage of entering into a trust deed is that all correspondence is directed to the trustee, who handles all of the communication with the creditors. There is no court involvement, unless the debtor refuses to cooperate with the trustee.

The arrangement is likely to lessen issues from creditors while all the associated interest and charges from unsecured debts (in the Trust Deed) are frozen (not if the debtor becomes able to pay interest prior to discharge). After 4 years your remainder of the debt can be written off. Only disposable income is used to pay creditors.

Disadvantages of a Trust Deed

The main disadvantage of a trust deed is that existing enforcement action, such as earning and bank arrestments may continue to be effective and home owners will be required to deal with equity in their home, should they have any. This can normally be dealt with without selling, although where there is an excessive amount of equity the debtor may be required to sell the property. Normally, equity can be dealt with by remortgaging, or extra monthly payments. The trust deed does not stop a person from being self-employed. While in the Protected Trust Deed, a person may not incur debt of more than £500.

A common misconception is that credit can continue to be used while in a trust deed, however, this could result in criminal charges. When entering a trust deed a default will be placed on the debtor's credit file which will last for six years. Some people are unable to sign a trust deed because their contract of employment states they cannot enter an insolvency solution. An individual's credit rating is negatively affected and trust deed is advertised in the *AIB register* - a public record.

Securing a trust deed

In order to enter such an agreement with your creditors, you must be a resident of Scotland. You need to consult the services of an Insolvency practitioner who will be able to explain all your options to you, based on your present financial situation. The qualified practitioner will evaluate your income to debt ratio such as mortgage, council tax, utility bills, and all other outgoings. Whatever is left from your earnings will be divided in equal proportions to pay towards your debts.

If, after learning how a Scottish trust deed works, you do decide to go ahead, the necessary paperwork will have to be signed and your trustee will try to protect your trust deed.

Obligations under a Trust Deed

When one agrees to enter into a trust deed, you take on the responsibilities and obligations of a regular legally binding contract to repay your debt. As such when one agrees to the terms of the trust deed you commit to:

Full cooperation with the trustee.
- To pay the agreed monthly contribution on time.
- To not enter into any additional credit agreements.
- To advise the trustee of any unexpected windfalls or payments or that your financial circumstances change.

Where, however, you experience a change in circumstances during your Trust Deed, such as unemployment, the trustee should review your finances to assess what is an appropriate level of contribution. This may mean you will only have to pay a reduced contribution or no contribution. Likewise, if during a Trust Deed your circumstances improve, one may be required to pay an increased monthly contribution.

Where one's circumstance change for the worse and you cannot maintain your level of contribution, although one may be allowed to pay a reduced contribution or no contribution you will still need to make arrangements to realise any equity in your property.

Where a trustee refuses to discharge the debtor at the end of the trust deed for failing to cooperate with the trustee, it may still be possible for the debtor to appeal to the sheriff for a discharge, especially where it can be shown they either didn't refuse to cooperate or couldn't reasonably be expected to.

Debt Management Programme

This is an informal arrangement between debtors and creditors to pay debts over an extended period of time. Debtors can arrange a programme directly with their creditors or with the help of a money adviser. Local money advisers can be found at Money Advice Scotland, or Citizens' Advice Scotland. Creditors do not have to agree to freeze interest or charges and can decide at any time that they no longer wish to accept payments and can pursue the debt using other methods.

Debt Arrangement Scheme

A Debt Arrangement Scheme, or DAS, is a statutory debt management scheme established by the Scottish Government and available to residents of Scotland. The debt arrangement scheme is an alternative solution to Trust Deeds in Scotland, and IVA's in England, allowing you to freeze the interest on your debts and repay over a period to suit you, whereas a Trust Deed would mean writing off substantial unaffordable debt. A key benefit of entering a DAS is that all interest, fees, penalties or charges on your debts are frozen and are waived when you complete your Debt Payment Programme (DPP). In addition, as long as you maintain payments to your mortgage and car you do not have to worry about losing them.

Another major advantage of a DAS is that it prevents creditors from taking legal action against you. In fact, you do not have to have any further direct contact with your creditors. This solution provides you with breathing space to allow you to focus on steadily repaying your debts rather than being contacted by your creditors or worrying about losing your home. It offers the opportunity of a fresh financial start as all of your debts included in a DAS will be fully paid at the end of the scheme.

What kinds of debt can be included in a DAS?

It is generally unsecured debt such as:
- ank and building society loans and overdrafts
- Credit cards, store cards and charge cards

- Home / online shopping catalogues
- Council Tax arrears
- Utility bill arrears

Mortgage debt is unlikely to be included as it is classed as a secured debt - i.e. your property is held as security against the loan. However, your monthly mortgage payment will be included when calculating your monthly DPP payment. If you have mortgage arrears you must contact your secured lender. If an agreement is reached with them arrears of mortgage payments can be included when calculating your monthly DPP payment.

How does a DAS work?

You need to consult a DAS approved Money Adviser who will make an application on your behalf. Individuals cannot make an application.

Your Money Adviser will have a confidential discussion with you about your financial position which will include details about your family, your income and expenditure, any assets you may have as well as the amount of your debts. This will help them calculate your disposable income to make a monthly payment to your creditors. Your Money Adviser will assess your position and will be able to inform you whether a DAS is the best option for you. Any fees charged and how these are deducted will be clearly explained to you. Once you decide that a DAS is the best option for you, your Money Adviser will submit an application for a DPP, contact your creditors for their approval.

Your creditors have twenty one days to respond to the application and if they do not respond they will be presumed to have consented. If one or more of your creditors object, the DPP will be considered by the DAS Administrator (The Accountant in Bankruptcy) and deems that the application is "fair and reasonable" they can legally force your creditors to comply with it.

Once approved you make an affordable monthly payment to an approved Payments Distributor. A monthly management fee is deducted and the balance is distributed to your creditors on a monthly basis. Your Creditors, not you, pay for the approved Payment Distribution service. Once you have made your last scheduled payment in terms of the DPP, all of your debts included in it will have been repaid in full. The duration of the DPP can vary according to individual circumstances - it can be as long as 10 years.

Advantages

- It prevents creditors from taking legal action against you.
- A Money Advisor deals with your creditors, relieving you of the stress.
- Interest, fees. Penalties or other charges are frozen from the date you apply for a DPP and are written off completely when it is completed.
- Your home will not be affected by the DAS as long as you maintain mortgage or rent payments on it.
- Sole traders may be able to include business debts in the DAS.
- Monthly payments are based on what you can reasonably afford to pay.
- If your circumstances change it may be possible to apply to vary the monthly payment amount and / or apply for a payment holiday of up to six months.

Disadvantages

- The DPP will last until your debts are repaid – there is no fixed time period.
- Arrears of secured debts cannot be included. The Money Adviser will assist you to make separate arrangements for these. Any repayments towards these will be classed as "ongoing liabilities" when calculating disposable income.
- Individuals cannot apply for a DAS - they must consult an Approved Money Advisor.
- Your credit rating may be affected if you enter a Debt Payment Programme and may affect your ability to obtain credit in the future.
- A DAS is only available to Scottish residents.

Business Debt Arrangement Scheme (BDAS)

The Business DAS extends the Debt Arrangement Scheme to a legal person, trust or unincorporated body of persons having an established place of business in Scotland or constituted or formed under Scots Law and at any time carrying on business in Scotland.

All debts for which an individual debtor is liable and a legal person, trust or unincorporated body persons is liable must be disclosed.

Useful addresses

Scotland's Financial Health Service

Further advice and information on dealing with personal debt can be obtained from the Scottish Government website – www.scotlandsfinancialhealthservice.gov.uk

For details on company insolvency in Scotland go to:

www.gov.uk/government/publications/liquidation-and-insolvency-companies-in-scotland

Accountancy in Bankruptcy-General enquiries

Tel: 0300 200 2600 if you wish to speak to someone about:

- a bankruptcy or bankruptcy application, a Protected Trust Deed or the Debt Arrangement Scheme
- ordering a publication or a discharge certificate
- if you want to speak to someone in a specific AiB team or if you are looking for information on the bankruptcy process or are unsure of who to speak to

Email with your enquiry or you can write to:

Accountant in Bankruptcy

1 Pennyburn Road

Kilwinning

KA13 6SA

Email: aib@aib.gsi.gov.uk

Debt Advisory Scotland (will advise on bankruptcy and the alternatives)

Phone: 0800 011 2322

Address:

Debt Advisory Services (Scotland) Limited

3 Stewart Street,

Milngavie,

Glasgow

G62 6BW

****

Chapter 9

Bankruptcy and Alternatives to Bankruptcy in Northern Ireland

---

Becoming bankrupt in Northern Ireland

The High Court in Belfast can declare you bankrupt by issuing a 'bankruptcy order' after it's been presented with a 'bankruptcy petition'.

A petition may be presented by:

- one or more creditors
- the debtor
- the supervisor of, or a person bound by, an individual voluntary agreement

Filing your own bankruptcy petition

If you decide that bankruptcy is the best option available to you there are a number of forms that you need to complete. You can get these forms, free of charge, from the Bankruptcy and Chancery Division of the High Court in Belfast or from the Insolvency Service:

- the petition (Insolvency Rules (NI) 1991 form 6.30) - this form is your request to the Court for you to be made bankrupt and includes the reasons for your request
- the statement of affairs (Insolvency Rules (NI) 1991 form 6.31) - this form asks you to list all your assets (anything

that belongs to you that may be used to pay your debts) and:

- o all your debts, including the names and addresses of the creditors and the amount you owe each one

When you have completed this form you will be asked to make a sworn statement as to its accuracy and completeness before an officer of the court or a solicitor - it is therefore vital that you make a full disclosure of your assets and debts

There are three fees that you will have to pay when you take your petition and statement of affairs to the Court. They are:

- the deposit of £525 towards the costs of administering your bankruptcy and is paid to the Department for the Economy - the deposit is payable in all cases and payment may be made in cash or postal orders or by a cheque from a building society, bank or solicitor - cheques should be made payable to the Official Receiver". Personal cheques will not be accepted

- the court fee of £144 - this fee may be paid in cash or by cheque or postal order made payable to 'Northern Ireland Courts and Tribunals Service' - in some circumstances the court may waive this fee; for example, if you are on Income Support. If you are not sure whether you qualify for a reduction in the fee or whether you are exempt from paying the fee, court staff will be able to advise you

- the fee payable to a solicitor before whom you swear the contents of your statement of affairs - you should expect to pay around £7 for this service

You should then take these completed forms, along with the receipt of your deposit paid to the Insolvency Service, to the High Court.

A creditor making you bankrupt

Your creditors can present a creditor's petition if you owe them an unsecured debt of over £5,000. This may be the sum of two or more debts which total over £5,000 and there may be different petitioning creditors on the same petition in respect of different debts.

Once bankruptcy proceedings have started, you must co-operate fully even if it's a creditor's petition and you dispute their claim. If possible you should try to reach a settlement before the petition's due to be heard - doing it later can be difficult and expensive.

Alternatives to bankruptcy

Bankruptcy is a serious matter - you'll have to give up possessions of value and the interest in your home. However, you don't have to become bankrupt just because you're in debt.

You can try to make arrangements with your creditors instead including:

- informal agreements - you write to your creditors and try to agree a repayment timetable
- individual voluntary arrangements (IVAs) - an insolvency practitioner helps you negotiate repayment terms

- administration orders - the Enforcement of Judgments Office (EJO) orders you to make payments, which the EJO then distributes amongst your creditors
- debt relief orders if you cannot pay and owe not more than £20,000

A Debt Relief Order is a formal insolvency process that is aimed at people who cannot pay their debts and who have no assets, a low income, no other access to debt relief and no prospect of the situation improving.

If people do have assets, or there is a possibility of an improvement in financial circumstances, a DRO is not an appropriate solution.

Where is a bankruptcy order made?

Bankruptcy petitions can only be presented in the High Court in Belfast.

Who deals with your bankruptcy?

Official Receiver

An Official Receiver is appointed to protect your assets. They act as trustee of your bankruptcy affairs if you have no assets.

Insolvency practitioner

If you do have assets, an Insolvency Practitioner will be appointed to act as trustee and sell your assets to pay your creditors. To find out more information visit:

Once a bankruptcy order has been made against you, your creditors can no longer pursue you for payment. Payment becomes the responsibility of the trustee.

How bankruptcy affects you

Assets

Once you're bankrupt, the Official Receiver, or appointed trustee, can sell your assets to pay your creditors. However, certain goods aren't treated as assets for this purpose, for example:

- equipment you need for your work (for example, tools or vehicles)
- household items needed by you and your family (for example, clothing, bedding and furniture)

If you own your home, you may have to sell the property. This will depend on who owns the property, the value of the home, and whether the property is worth more than your mortgage. This is called 'equity'. It may be possible for the joint owner or family and friends to make an offer to the official receiver to buy out your share of the equity. This is particularly helpful if there is little or no equity.

Earnings

The Official Receiver can look at your income (taking into account expenses such as your mortgage, rent and household bills) and decide if payments should be made to your creditors.

You may be asked to sign an 'income payments agreement' to pay fixed monthly instalments from your income for three years. If you don't pay (or if you don't sign the agreement voluntarily), the Official Receiver can apply for an income payments order from the court to order you to pay. This will run for at least three years from the date of the order.

If your circumstances change, you'll need to tell the Official Receiver, so they can review these arrangements.

Ongoing commitments

You'll still have to meet ongoing commitments such as rent or debts incurred after you become bankrupt.

Other applications

The Official Receiver or a trustee in bankruptcy can make other applications to the Court following a Bankruptcy Order. They include:

- public examinations
- applications to suspend automatic discharge
- applications for permission to act a a director
- private examinations

Your obligations when you're bankrupt

You must:

- give the Official Receiver details of your finances, assets and creditors
- look after your assets and hand them over to the Official Receiver with the relevant paperwork, such as bank statements and insurance policies
- tell your trustee (either the Official Receiver or insolvency practitioner) about any new assets or income during your bankruptcy
- stop using credit cards and bank or building society accounts
- not obtain credit over £500 without telling the creditor that you're bankrupt not make payments direct to your

creditors (there are exceptions to this, such as mortgage arrears and outstanding child support payments)

You may be able to open a basic bank account once you are bankrupt. Even after the bankruptcy period, you may find it difficult to obtain credit. The Official Receiver does not send any form of notice to credit reference agencies.

The agencies pick up information from other sources such as the Insolvency Register, advertisements of bankruptcies in newspapers, "The Belfast Gazette" and the "Belfast Telegraph", and the Enforcement of Judgements Office.

Details of your bankruptcy are also kept on the Insolvency Register which is maintained by the Bankruptcy and Chancery Office at the High Court and contains records of all insolvencies in Northern Ireland for the last ten years.

How long does bankruptcy last?
Bankruptcy normally lasts for one year. After this time, you'll be 'discharged' from your bankruptcy regardless of how much you still owe. Your discharge could happen earlier if you co-operate fully with the Official Receiver. However, in a small number of cases and if you've behaved irresponsibly (for example, by not cooperating), bankruptcy can last for much more than one year.

Useful information and advice
If you're thinking about declaring yourself bankrupt or you're being threatened with bankruptcy, or wish to pursue one of the other arrangements available, such as an Idnivual Voluntary Arrangement, it's important to seek independent advice. Several agencies offer free help including:

Citizens Advice Northern Ireland www.citizensadvice.co.uk

Step Change Debt Charity www.stepchange.org 0800 138 1111

Advice NI www.nidirect.gov.uk

Debt advice Northern Ireland www.
debtadvicenorthernireland.co.uk 0800 043 0550

****

Glossary of terms

Administration order-this is an order made in a county court to arrange and administer the payment of debts by an individual.

Annulment-cancellation.

Assets-anything that belongs to a debtor that may be used to pay off debts.

Bankrupt-a person against whom a bankruptcy order has been made by a court.

Bankruptcy-the process of dealing with the estate of a bankrupt

Bankruptcy restriction notice-a notice entered at the Land Registry on any property involved in a bankruptcy.

Bankruptcy order-a court order making an individual bankrupt.

Bankruptcy petition- a request made to the court for a debtor to be made bankrupt.

Bankruptcy restrictions order or undertaking- a procedure whereby the restrictions of bankruptcy continue to apply for between 2-15 years.

Charging order- an order made by the court giving the trustee a legal charge on the bankrupt's property for the amount owed.
Creditor-someone who is owed money by a bankrupt.

Creditor's committee- a committee representing the interests of all creditors in supervising the activities of a trustee in bankruptcy.

Debt Arrangement Scheme-An alternative to bankruptcy in Scotland.

Debt Management Plan-an informal arrangement negotiated with creditors by an independent company.

Debt Relief Order-an alternative to bankruptcy for smaller debts.

Debtor-someone who owes money.

Discharge-free from bankruptcy.

Estate-assets or property of the bankrupt which the trustee can use to pay creditors.

Fast Track Voluntary Arrangement-a voluntary agreement with creditors to pay all or part of the money owed, which can only be entered into when bankrupt.

Income payment agreements (IPA) a written agreement where the bankrupt voluntarily agrees to pay the trustee part of his or her income for an agreed period.

Income payments order (IPO)-where the court orders the bankrupt to pay part of their income to the trustee for a period.

Individual Voluntary Arrangement (IVA)-a voluntary arrangement for an individual where a compromise scheme for payment of debts is put to creditors.

Insolvency-being unable to pay debts when they are due.

Insolvency practitioner-an authorised person specialising in insolvency, usually a solicitor or accountant.

Nominee-an insolvency practitioner who carries out the preparatory work for a voluntary arrangement.

Non-provable debt-debt which is not included in the bankruptcy proceedings. An individual remains liable for such debt regardless of his or her bankruptcy.

Official receiver-a civil servant and officer of the court employed by the Insolvency Service, which deals with bankruptcies.

Petition-a formal application made to court by the debtor or creditor.

Preferential creditor-a creditor entitled to receive certain payments in priority to other unsecured creditors.

Public examination-where the Official receiver questions the bankrupt in open court.

Secured creditor-a creditor holding security, such as a mortgage.

Secured creditor-a charge or mortgage over assets taken to secure the payment of a debt. Where the debt is not paid, the lender has the right to sell the charged assets.

Statement of affairs-a document completed by a bankrupt and sworn under oath, stating the assets and giving details of debtors and creditors.

Sequestration-The process of bankruptcy in Scotland

Trustee-either the Official Receiver or an insolvency practitioner who takes control over the assets of a bankrupt.

Trust deed-an alternative to bankruptcy in Scotland

Unsecured creditor-a creditor who does not hold any security for money owed.

Unsecured debt-a debt owed to an unsecured creditor.
****

Useful Addresses and Websites

Bankruptcy Information Centre
bankruptcy.org.uk
03335 77 88 79

Business Debtline (BDL) is a charity which offers free, impartial and confidential advice to businesses in financial difficulty in the UK both on its website and by a helpline.
Business Debtline- Freephone: 0800 197 6026 (Monday to Friday from 9am to 5pm) Website: www.bdl.org.uk

Insolvency Service
https://www.gov.uk/government/organisations/insolvency-service
0300 678 0015

Citizens Advice Bureau
www.citizensadvice.org.uk

Community Legal Services
www.clsdirect.org.uk

Step Change Charity (formerly Consumer Credit Counselling Service). Step Change is a registered charity dedicated to providing free, confidential counselling and money management help to families and individuals in financial distress. Step change deals with the whole of the UK.
Helpline 0800 138 1111
www.stepchange.org

National Debtline

National Debtline provides free confidential and independent advice over the telephone for anyone in financial difficulties.

Helpline 0808 808 4000

www.nationaldebtline.co.uk

For Scotland and Ireland see respective chapters 8 and 9.

****

Index

Administration, 5, 21, 55, 67, 68, 69, 70, 71
Administration Order, 5, 55, 67, 68, 69, 70, 71
Annulment, 137
Assets, 7, 75, 108, 137

Bankruptcy, 3, 6, 17, 83, 109, 137, 140
Benefit overpayments, 75
Buy now-pay later agreements, 75

Call Credit, 109
Certificate of Satisfaction, 70, 71
Child support, 75
Citizens Advice Bureau, 58, 74, 141
Company Directors Disqualifications Act 1986, 17
Composition order, 67, 71
Composition Order, 67, 69, 71
Council tax, 69, 75
Court fines, 75
COVID 19, 11
Credit cards, 56
Credit reference agencies, 8, 109
Creditors, 58, 76

Data Protection Act 1988, 109
Debt Management Plan, 5, 55, 56, 57, 138
Debt Management Plans, 5, 55, 56
Debt Relief Orders, 5, 11, 73
Debt Relief Restriction Order, 78, 79
Debt Respite Scheme 2021, 12
Debts, 5, 7, 69, 108, 109
Department of Business, Innovation and Skills, 17

Employment Rights Act 1996, 17

Ending bankruptcy, 7, 107
Enterprise Act 2002, 17
Equifax, 109
Experian, 109

Fast Track Voluntary Arrangement, 6, 83, 138

Hire purchase or conditional sale agreements, 75
HM Revenue and Customs, 105
Household equipment, 76

Income Payments Agreement, 106
Income Payments Order, 106
Index, 9, 142
Individual Insolvency Register, 77
Individual Voluntary Arrangement, 55, 61, 76, 139
Individual Voluntary Arrangements, 5, 11, 12, 61
Information Commissioner, 110
Insolvency Service, 3, 6, 17, 19, 20, 73, 77, 86, 89, 90, 100, 101,
    129, 131, 139
Interest, 126

Law Society, 73
Licensed Insolvency Practitioner, 61, 62
Licensed Insolvency Practitioners, 61
Life insurance policy, 7, 106
London Gazette, 86, 91

Mental health crisis breathing space ends, 4, 50

Official Receiver, 3, 19, 20, 77, 78, 79, 84, 108, 140
Overdrafts, 56, 75

Pension rights, 7, 105
Personal loans, 56

Public examination, 7, 92

Registry of County Court Judgements, 70
Rent, 75
Restrictions on a bankrupt, 7, 106

Secured borrowing, 56
Social fund loans, 75
Standard breathing space, 3, 4, 12, 23, 25, 27, 44, 45, 46, 49
Store cards, 56
Student loans, 56, 75

Telephone, 75
The Insolvency Service, 3, 17, 19
Tools, 76

Utilities, 75

Wages, 7, 106

Your home, 7, 104

****

Appendix 1 Various forms used in personal bankruptcy in the UK. For a full list of forms go to: https://www.gov.uk/government/collections/court-and-tribunal-forms

1. Application for an Administration Order

2. Administration Order-Notes for Guidance

3. Certificate for Sequestration (Scotland)

4. Income and expenditure form for Trust Deed (Scotland)

5. Debtors Bankruptcy Petition (Northern Ireland)

Application for an administration order

Please read the notes for guidance (form N270) before completing this form. Complete all details in black ink.

Name of court

Application no.
(For court use only)

Part A - Statement of means

Please complete the following statement of means as fully as possible. Continue on a separate sheet if necessary.

1. Personal details

Full name

Address (including postcode)

Mr ☐   Mrs ☐   Miss ☐   Ms ☐

Married ☐   Civil partner ☐   Single ☐   Other ☐

Date of birth D D M M Y Y Y Y

2. Dependants *(people you look after financially)*

Number of children in each age group

under 11 ☐   11-15 ☐   16-17 ☐   18 and over ☐

Other dependants *(give details)*

3. Bank/Building society accounts and savings

☐ I have a current account

☐ The account is in **credit** by £

☐ The account is **overdrawn** by £

☐ I have a savings or deposit account

☐ The amount in the account is £

I have other savings or investments *(give details)*

4. Employment

Complete all the boxes that apply. If you are not in paid employment and are not seeking work eg. a homemaker, you should say so in the unemployment section.

☐ I am employed as a

My employer (including full address)

My works number and/or pay reference

Jobs other than main job *(give details)*

☐ I have been unemployed for *(say how long)*

Do you have any reason to believe that you may be able to obtain employment within the next three months?

☐ I am self employed as a

Give details of:
a) contracts and other work in hand

b) any sums due for work done

£

☐ I receive a pension

5. Property

I live in

jointly owned property ☐   my own property ☐   lodgings ☐

rented property ☐   other eg. with parents ☐

amount due under a mortgage/ charges against property £

value of property £

N92 Application for an Administration Order (Order 35, rule 2(1) (04.06)   HMC

Statement of means - income and expenditure

Important: It will help the court if you give all sums for income and expenditure as either monthly or weekly figures. Try not to mix the two.

Income - See page 2 of the notes for guidance before completing this section

	specify weekly/monthly		specify weekly/monthly
My usual take home pay	£	→sub total brought forward	£ 0.00
My partner contributes to the expenses listed in section 7	£	Income support (see notes for guidance)	£
Others living in my home give me	£	Child benefit(s)	£
My pension(s)	£	Other state benefits	
er income (give details)			£
	£		£
Sub total	£ 0.00	**Total**	£ 0.00

Regular expenses and arrears

e page 3 of the notes for guidance ore completing any part of this ction	**(a) Regular payments** Enter the amount you usually spend or must pay for each item, weekly or monthly (please complete each entry: write n/a if not applicable) *weekly/monthly*	**(b) Total arrears** If you are in arrears with any of the items in the regular payments column(a), enter the total arrears owed in column (b). Full details should be given in the list of creditors (see notes for guidance).	**(c) Regular arrears payments** If you are paying off the arrears shown in column (b) show much you are paying weekly or monthly in column (c). Do not include these amounts as regular payments in column (a). *weekly/monthly*
Rent	£	£	£
Mortgage/home loan	£	£	£
Second mortgage/secured loan	£	£	£
Life insurance/endowment	£	£	£
House contents insurance	£	£	£
Council tax/community charge arrears	£	£	£
Maintenance/child support	£	£	£
Water/sewerage charges	£	£	£
Ground rent/service charge	£	£	£
Gas (or other fuel eg coal, oil)	£	£	£
Electricity	£	£	£
TV rental / licence	£	£	£
Magistrates' Court fine(s)	£	£	£
SS Social Fund Loan/overpaid benefit	£	£	£
phone *(line, phone rental, essential calls only)*	£	£	£
Child care	£	£	£
Food and household essentials	£	£	£
Clothing	£	£	£
Laundry	£	£	£
elling expenses *(essential eg work, school)*	£	£	£
School meals/meals at work	£	£	£
Prescriptions/dentists/optician	£	£	£

Others *(eg hire purchase) see guidance notes*

	(a)	(b)	(c)
	£	£	£
	£	£	£
	£	£	£
	7a Total expenses	**7b Total arrears**	
	£0.00 per w/m	£0.00	£0.00

Part B - List of creditors *(see page 4 of the notes for guidance)*

Applicant's name	Application no. *(For court use only)*	

Name of creditor, if known, and address to which payment should be sent. Give reference/account number. If judgment debt, also state court and case number *(see example 3 in notes for guidance).*	If someone else is jointly responsible for part of this debt give details (eg. guarantor, joint account etc.)	Amount outstanding	
		£	p
		Sub total	

ame of creditor, if known, and address to which payment hould be sent. Give reference/account number. If judgment ebt, also state court and case number	If someone else is jointly responsible for part of this debt give details (eg. guarantor, joint account etc.)	Amount outstanding	
		£	p
	Sub total brought forward		
	Total		

continue on a separate sheet if necessary

art C - Offer of payment

ou do not have to make an offer of payment as the court will fix a rate r you to pay based on the information you have given on this form. you do make an offer, it should be one you can afford to pay.

offer to pay by instalments of

£ _____ per week/month

☐ **Please tick if you object to the court making an attachment of earnings order and give your reasons in the space opposite** *(see notes for guidance).*

If you wish the court to take anything else into account when making an order, please give details *(see notes for guidance).*

art D - Declaration *(to be signed and sworn or affirmed before an officer of the court)*

efore you sign this form take it to the court office with a copy of the judgment or order *(see notes for guidance)*

I ask the court to make an administration order.

_____ (full name)

of _____ (address)

declare on oath/affirm that to the best of my knowledge, the names of all creditors, and the debts I owe them, are truly recorded in the list of creditors and that the information I have given in my application and the statement of means is true.

_____ Signature

worn/affirmed at:

the County of _____ this _____ day of _____ 20___

efore me

fficer of the court, appointed by the Judge to take affidavits pursuant to s.58 of the County Courts Act 1984

Administration orders

Notes for guidance

Please read these notes carefully. The notes will help you decide if you qualify for an administration order. They will also help you to complete the application (form N92).

What is an administration order?

If you are in financial difficulties and you are unable to pay your creditors (the people you owe money to) an administration order may help you.

- An administration order allows you to pay a sum that you can afford into the court each month to cover all your debts.

- In some circumstances the court may make an order for you to pay less than the total you owe (a 'composition order'). This may be appropriate if it is clear that you will not be able to pay your debts in full in a reasonable period (say three years). You may ask the court to consider this by using the box in part C on the application form – but the final decision is for the court.

- The court will divide your monthly payment among your creditors (in proportion to the size of each debt).

- The court will manage your debts and deal directly with your creditors.

- While the order is in force none of the creditors named in your application or in the schedule to the order may try to enforce the debt or try to make you bankrupt (insolvent) without first asking the court.

- You will not need to pay a fee when you make the application. But, if an order is made, the court will deduct a sum for its costs from each of the payments you make. This is currently 10 pence in every £1 paid. For example, if you pay £20 each month, £2 will be paid to the court. To put it another way, if your total payments amount to £2,000 you will pay an additional sum of £200 to the court during the life of the order.

Do I qualify for an administration order?

To qualify for an administration order

- You must have two or more outstanding debts. At least one debt must be a High Court or county court judgment.

- Your total debts as stated on the list of creditors must not be more than £5,000.

If you satisfy these requirements, you may qualify for an administration order. If you do not qualify or you think you may qualify but need further advice, you should contact your local citizens advice bureau, money advice centre or legal advice centre.

What happens to my application?

- The court will look at your income and expenditure and consider your offer before fixing a rate of payment. This will normally be done without the need for a hearing and you and your creditors will have 16 days in which to write to the court with any objection

- If there are no objections, an order will be made in t terms proposed by the court. You will be told how a when to pay the court.

- If you or any of your creditors object, or the court has difficulty in setting a rate of payment, you will be told to come to court for a hearing before the district judge.

- A creditor may object to their debt being included in the administration order. If the court agrees, the creditor will not be able to take action against you separately to recover the debt without first asking th court.

- If you are employed, the court may order your employer to send deductions direct from your earnings to the court. This is called an attachment of earnings order. If you object to this, you **must** tick the box in part C. You must give good reasons for objecting. The court may make a suspended attachment of earnings order. This means that as lo as you regularly pay the administration order, your employer will not be asked to make deductions from your earnings. But if you do not keep up payments, the court may send the order to your employer without telling you.

- If an administration order is made, it will be registere in the Register of Judgments, Orders and Fines. Thi will make it difficult for you to get credit. When the order is paid in full, you can ask the court to mark th entry in the Register as satisfied and for a certificate proving payment. You will need to pay a fee for this.

- County court judgments included in the list of creditors may be registered separately. Court staff w be able to tell you how to have these entries on the Register marked satisfied.

What happens if I am unable to keep up the payments?

- If you cannot keep up payments **you must contact the court immediately.** The court may be able to help you. It is important that you do not get deeper into debt.

- If you do not pay once the order has been made, the court may send the bailiff to take and sell your possessions, or make an attachment of earnings order to enforce payment. Alternatively, it may revok (cancel) the order and your creditors will be able to take action against you separately to recover their debts.

ow do I complete e application form?

ase read these guidance notes carefully before you mplete the application form for an administration order m N92).

Complete the application form and details of your income (section 6) and expenditure (section 7) as fully as possible. See the examples and notes below to help you complete the form. The court will use this information to fix the amount you will be expected to pay.

It will help the court if you give all sums for income and expenditure as either monthly or weekly – try not to mix the two.

Completing Section 6 – income

- Complete details of all your income (section 6) as fully as possible.

- If you receive income from a second job or you regularly earn overtime you should show this in the 'other income' box.

- If you receive Income Support you should enter the figure you actually receive after any deductions are made.

- If you receive any other benefits (eg disablement benefit) you should say so and show how much you receive in 'the other benefits' box.

- If your partner contributes to or pays any of the expenses in box 7, you must include the amount they pay in box 6.

- If you are in arrears with national insurance or income tax you should not deduct these from your take home pay. Instead, your should list them in section 7.

Example 1

Statement of means - income and expenditure
◆ Important: It will help the court if you give all sums for income and expenditure as either monthly or weekly figures. Try not to mix the two.

6. Income

See page 2 of the notes for guidance before completing this section

	specify weekly/monthly			*specify weekly/monthly*	
My usual take home pay	£905	per month	Sub total brought forward	£1105	per month
My partner contributes to the expenses listed in section 7	£100	per month	Income support *(see notes for guidance)*	£ —	
Others living in my home give me	£ —		Child benefit(s)	£41	per month
My pension(s)	£ —		Other state benefits *(specify)*		
Other income *(give details)*			none	£	
overtime	£100	per month		£	
Sub total	£1105	per month	Total	£1146	per month

2

Completing Section 7 – expenditure

- You should list all the money you regularly pay out each month in regular expenses and arrears (section 7). List all the regular payments you make in column (a).

  If you are in arrears with any of these items, eg unpaid rent, you should list the total amount of the arrears you owe in column (b). Full details must also be given in the list of creditors (part B).

- If you are paying the arrears off by instalments, for example at a rate agreed with the creditor or under a court order, you should say how much you pay each week or month in column (c).
  Do not include this amount in column (a).

- If any amounts are deducted directly from your income (eg an attachment of earnings order for council tax or maintenance) or your benefit (eg refund of social fund loan or overpaid benefit) you should not include these sums anywhere in section 7. You must include them in the schedule and say that they are deducted direct from your income.

- Council tax has now replaced community charge. You should enter the amount you pay regularly for council tax in column (a), and any arrears or arrears of community charge under column (b) and (c).

- If you include travelling expenses in the regular expenses column you should only include expenses for bus or train fares or petrol. You should not include expenses for car insurance or road fund licence.

- If you make regular payments for items that are not listed, say what they are in the boxes marked 'others'. Examples might be repayment of a loan, hire purchase instalments or regular credit card payments.

Example 2

7. Regular expenses and arrears

See page 3 of the notes for guidance before completing any part of this section

	(a) Regular payments		(b) Total arrears	(c) Regular arrears payments	
	Enter the amount you usually spend or must pay for each item, weekly or monthly (please complete each entry: write n/a if not applicable)		If you are in arrears with any of the items in the regular payments column (a), enter the total arrears owed in column (b). Full details should be given in the list of creditors (see notes for guidance)	If you are paying off the arrears shown in column (b) show how much you are paying weekly or monthly in column (c). Do not include these amounts as regular payments in column (a).	
	weekly monthly			weekly monthly	
Rent	£500	per month	£	£	
Mortgage/home loan	£ n/a		£	£	
Second mortgage/secured loan	£ n/a		£	£	
Life insurance/endowment	£20	per month	£	£	
House contents insurance	£60	per month	£	£	
Council tax/community charge arrears	£40	per month	£	£	
Maintenance/child support	£200	per month	£600	£40	per month
Water/sewerage charges	£16	per month	£	£	
Ground rent/service charge	£ n/a		£	£	
Gas (or other fuel eg coal, oil)	£30 gas	per month	£	£	
Electricity	£15	per month	£150	£10	per month
TV rental / licence	£6	per month	£	£	
Magistrates' Court fine(s)	£ n/a		£	£	
DSS Social Fund Loan/overpaid benefit	£ n/a		£	£	
Telephone (line, phone rental, essential calls only)	£10	per month	£	£	
Child care	£ n/a		£	£	
Food and household essentials	£150	per month	£	£	
Clothing	£5	per month	£	£	
Laundry	£ n/a		£	£	
Travelling expenses (essential eg work, school)	£15	per month	£	£	
School meals/meals at work	£ n/a		£	£	
Prescriptions/dentists/optician	£ n/a		£	£	

Others (eg hire purchase) (see notes for guidance)

	(a)		(b)	(c)	
Bank overdraft	£5	per month	£200	£	
H.P (3 piece suite)	£10	per month	£50	£5	per month
Visa card	£50	per month	£500	£	

7a Total expenses	7b Total arrears
£1132 per w/m	£1500

You must list all your debts in the list of creditors (you may be required to provide proof of each debt) and say what each debt is for (see the examples below).

- **At least one debt must be a High Court or county court judgment debt.** Remember to give the name of the court and case numbers for any county court or High Court debts (see example below). You must also provide a copy of the judgment or order, summons or writ.

ample 3

Part B: list of creditors *(see page 4 of the notes for guidance)*

Applicant's name JOHN SLOPE		Application Number	For court use only		

Name of creditor, if known, and address to which payment should be sent. Give reference/account number. If judgment debt, also state court and case number *(see example 3 in notes for guidance)*	If someone else is jointly responsible for part of this debt give details (eg guarantor, joint account etc)	Amount outstanding	
		£	p
1 Furniture for you'ltd (for 3 piece suite) ref 7365 27161 PH Pliwood House Barchester, Barsetshire Case no. 9210144 Barchester County Court		362	97
2 Grantley Bank PLC (overdraft) A/c 217/1894/202 30 High Street Barchester Barsetshire	Mrs O Slope (joint account)	200	00
3 Midlays visa card A/c 3491/4320/6191/7723 29 Old View Barchester, Barsetshire		500	00
4 3 Bonds Sportswear (bounced cheque) 2 High Street Barchester, Barsetshire Payable to: EM Wentworth (Solicitor) ref EMW/DTM 15 High Street Barchester Barsetshire		27	34

hould I make an offer of ayment?

You may wish to suggest a rate at which you could pay back your debts (see part C of the application form). You do not have to make an offer but, if you do, it should be one you can afford to pay (however small).

If you are employed, the court may ask your employer to send deductions direct from your earnings to the court. This is called an attachment of earnings order. If you object to this, you must tick the box in part C and say why you object. If you do not give good reasons, the court will consider making an order.

What should I do with the completed application form?

- Take the unsigned completed application form to your local county court. You will be asked to sign the form in front of a court officer and you will have to swear on oath that the information given in your application is true. If you can, bring any bills, statements and invoices to support the details of your income and expenditure.

- If you need help to complete the application form (N92) you should ask at your local county court office, citizens advice bureau, money advice centre or legal advice centre.

- **Take a photocopy of the completed application you may need to refer to it.**

Form 2

Certificate for Sequestration

Bankruptcy (Scotland) Act 2016
Section 9

This certificate is invalid unless----

- Completed by a money adviser defined in section 4(2) of the Bankruptcy (Scotland) Act 2016, and
- Countersigned by the debtor.

This certificate is valid for 30 days including the date signed by the money adviser.

I,	Insert money adviser's name
	Job title
	Organisation
	Address
	Town
	Postcode
	e-mail address
	Phone number

confirm that, under sections 4(2) and 9(1) of the Bankruptcy (Scotland) Act 2016, I am a money adviser who may grant this certificate which has been applied for by the debtor, and certified that, on the basis of the information provided to me, by

	Insert debtor's name and title
	Address
	Town
	Postcode
	Telephone number
	Date of birth

that he/she* is unable to pay his/her* debts as they become due.

I have provided the debtor with a copy of the Debt Advice and Information Pack and, where appropriate, have advised the debtor of the options of a voluntary repayment plan, a debt payment programme under the Debt Arrangement Scheme or Trust Deed.

I have advised the debtor that an award of sequestration, if granted, is recorded in a public register and may result in one or more of the following:

1) the debtor being refused credit, or being offered credit at a higher rate, whether before or after the date of the debtor being discharged;
2) the debtor not being able to remain in his/her current place of residence;
3) the debtor being required to relinquish property which they own;
4) the debtor being required to make contributions from income for the benefit of creditors;
5) damage to the debtor's business interests and employment prospects;
6) the debtor still being liable for some debts which are excluded;
7) the debtor's past financial transactions being investigated; and
8) other restrictions or requirements imposed on the debtor as a result of the debtor's own circumstances and actions.

Please select the relevant qualification which gives you the authority to grant a certificate for sequestration.

☐ person qualified to act as insolvency practitioner in relation to individuals in accordance with section 390 of the Insolvency Act 1986 (c.45)
☐ person who works for such an insolvency practitioner, and who has been given authority by that insolvency practitioner to act on behalf of that insolvency practitioner in providing money advice.
☐ person who works as money adviser for organisations which have been awarded accreditation at type 2 level or above against the Scottish National Standards for Information and Advice Provision
☐ person approved for the purpose of the Debt Arrangement Scheme
☐ person who works as a money adviser for citizens advice bureau which is a full member of the Scottish Association of Citizens Advice Bureaux/Citizens Advice Scotland
☐ person who works as money adviser for a local authority in Scotland

Signed _____(money adviser) _____(date)

I, _____ (debtor's name) confirm that I have provided the money adviser with correct and complete information about my financial circumstances.

Signed _____ (debtor) _____(date)

Form 2A   Regulation 10(1)(d)(ii)

INCOME AND EXPENDITURE

The Protected Trust Deed (Scotland) Regulations 2013

Debtor's Name:
AiB Reference Number:

Salary and Wages

Income	Amount (£)	Frequency
Debtor's salary/wages		
Partner's salary/wages		

Total

Pensions

Pension(s)	Amount (£)	Frequency
State Pension(s)		
Private or work pension(s)		
Pension Credit		

Total

Other income

Other income	Amount (£)	Frequency
Maintenance or child support		
Boarders or lodgers		
Non-dependant contribution		
Student loan or grants		
(to be completed with any other household income)		

Total

Benefits

Type of benefit	Amount (£)	Frequency
Jobseeker's Allowance		
Income Support		
Working Tax Credits		
Child Tax Credits		
Employment and Support Allowance		
DLA, PIP or Attendance Allowance		
Carer's Allowance		
Housing Benefit/Local Housing Allowance		
Council Tax Reduction		
Universal Credit		
(other)		
(other)		
(other)		

Total

Please use the space provided below to give details of any benefit listed under "other"

Expenditure

Essential expenditure	Amount (£)	Frequency
Rent		
Ground rent, service charges, factor fees		
Mortgages		
Other Secured Loans		
Building and Content Insurance		
Pension and Life insurance		
Council Tax		
Gas		
Electricity		
TV Licence		
Magistrates or Sheriff Court Fines		
Maintenance or Child Support		
Hire Purchase/Conditional Sales		
Childcare Costs		
Adult Care Costs		

Total

Phone	Amount (£)	Frequency
Home Phone		
Mobile Phone(s)		

Total

Travel	Amount (£)	Frequency
Public Transport (work, school, shopping, etc.)		
Car Insurance		
Vehicle Tax		
Fuel (petrol, diesel, oil, etc.)		
MOT and car maintenance		
Breakdown and Recovery		
Parking charges or Tolls		

Total

Housekeeping	Amount (£)	Frequency
Food and Milk		
Cleaning and Toiletries		
Newspapers and Magazines		
Cigarettes, Tobacco and Sweets		
Alcohol		
Laundry and dry cleaning		
Clothing and Footwear		
Nappies and baby items		
Pet Food		

Total

Other expenditure	Amount (£)	Frequency
Health (dentist, glasses, prescriptions, health insurance)		
Repairs/house maintenance (including window cleaning, maintenance contracts)		
Hairdressing/haircuts		
Cable, Satellite and Internet		
TV, video and other appliance rental		
School meals and meals at work		
Pocket money and school trips		
Lottery and Pools etc.		
Hobbies/leisure/sport (include pub, outings, etc.)		
Gifts (Christmas, Birthday, Charity, etc.)		
Vet Bills and Pet Insurance		

Total

All other expenses not covered above	Amount (£)	Frequency

Total

Total Income

Total Expenditure

Surplus Income

Statements:

I certify that this is a full disclosure of my Income and Expenditure:

Debtor Signature _____ Date

I confirm that in accordance with Regulation 11 (1)(h) of the Protected Trust Deeds (Scotland) Regulations 2013 (as amended), I have assessed the debtor's contribution in accordance with Common Financial Tool (CFT) and the CFT has been used in this calculation.

I confirm that the Common Financial Statement (CFS) trigger figures have been used in this calculation and have not been exceeded. *

The Common Financial Statement (CFS) trigger figures have been exceeded in the following category/categories and the reason(s) are: *

* Delete as appropriate

I confirm that Common Financial Statement (CFS) allowances for dependant(s) and/or vehicle(s), that have been used in this calculation, have not to the best of my knowledge and belief, been replicated in any other income and expenditure assessment carried out in respect of a trust deed for any other individual.

Trustee Signature _____ Date

Rule 6.034   Form 6.30

Debtor's Bankruptcy Petition

No. _____

IN THE HIGH COURT OF JUSTICE IN NORTHERN IRELAND
CHANCERY DIVISION (BANKRUPTCY)

* Insert title

(a) Insert full
name, address and
occupation (if
any) of debtor

(b) Insert in full
any other name(s)
by which the
debtor is or has
been known

(c) Insert former
address or
addresses at
which the debtor
may have incurred
debts or liabilities
still unpaid or
unsatisfied

(d) Insert trading
name (adding
"with another or
others", if this is
so), business
address and nature
of the business

(e) Insert any
former trading
names (adding
"with another or
others", if this is
so), business
address and nature
of the business in
respect of which
the debtor may
have incurred
debts or liabilities
still unpaid or
unsatisfied

(f) Delete as
applicable

Re*

I (a)

also known as (b)

[lately residing at (c) _____]

[and carrying on business as (d) _____]

[and lately carrying on business as (e) _____]

request the court that a bankruptcy order be made against me and say as follows:--

1. (f) My centre of main interests, being the place where I conduct the administration of my interests, is located within the United Kingdom, at

OR

My centre of main interests is located outside the United Kingdom but within the European Union and I have an establishment as defined by EC Regulation No. 1346/2000 within Northern Ireland at

OR

My centre of main interests is located outside the European Union.

OR

I carry on business as an insurance undertaking; a credit institution; investment undertaking providing services involving the holding of funds or securities for third parties; or a collective investment undertaking as referred to in Article 1.2 of the EC Regulation.

2. (f) The proceedings will be main OR secondary OR territorial proceedings for the purposes of the EC Regulation.

OR

The proceedings do not fall within the EC Regulation.

Under the EC Regulation
- (i) Centre of main interests should correspond to the place where the debtor conducts the administration of his interests on a regular basis.
- (ii) Establishment is defined in the Council Regulation (No. 1346/2000) on insolvency proceedings as "any place of operations where the debtor carries out a non-transitory economic activity with human means and goods"

3. I am unable to pay my debts.

4. (f) That within the period of five years ending with date of this petition: –

(i) I have not been adjudged bankrupt

OR

I was adjudged bankrupt on (g) _____ in the High Court of Justice in Northern Ireland

Record No.

    (ii) I have not (f) [made a composition with my creditors in satisfaction of my debts] or (f) [entered into a scheme of arrangement with creditors]

OR

On (g) _____ I (f) [made a composition] [entered into a scheme of arrangement] with my creditors.

(iii) I have not entered into a voluntary arrangement.

OR

On (g) _____ I entered into a voluntary arrangement.

(iv) I have not been subject to an administration order under Article 80 of the Judgments Enforcement (Northern Ireland) Order 1981

OR

On (g) _____ an administration order was made against me in the Enforcement of Judgments Office.

5. A statement of my affairs is filed with this petition.

Date

Signature

Complete only if petition not heard immediately

Endorsement

This petition having been presented to the court on _____ it is ordered that the petition shall be heard as follows:–

Date

Time   hours

Place
